Cultures and Politics

Socialist History 18

Rivers Oram Press
London, Sydney and New York

Editorial Team
Kevin Morgan
Stephen Woodhams
Willie Thompson
David Parker
Mike Waite
David Morgan
Heather Williams
Julie Johnson

Editorial Advisors
Noreen Branson
Rodney Hilton
Eric Hobsbawm
David Howell
Monty Johnstone
Victor Kiernan
David Marquand
Ben Pimlott
Pat Thane

All editorial enquiries to Kevin Morgan, Department of Government, University of Manchester M13 9PL or Kevin.Morgan@man.ac.uk

Published in 2000
by Rivers Oram Press, an imprint of Rivers Oram Publishers Ltd
144 Hemingford Road, London N1 1DE

Distributed in the USA by
New York University Press, 838 Broadway, New York, NY 10003–4183

Distributed in Australia and New Zealand by
UNIReps, University of New South Wales, Sydney, NSW 2052

Set in Garamond by
NJ Design Associates
and printed in Great Britain by
T.J. International Ltd, Padstow

British Library Cataloguing in Publication Data
A catalogue record for this publication is available from the British Library
ISBN 1 85489 122 7 (hb)
ISBN 1 85489 123 5 (pb)
ISSN 0969 4331

Contents

Women's suffrage
Cheryl Law, *Suffrage and Power: The women's movement 1918–1928*
(Christine Jackson)

Imagining otherness
Rana Kabbani, *Imperial Fictions. Europe's myths of Orient* (Kathy Burton)

Creating history
Jane McDermid and Anna Hillyar, *Midwives of the Revolution. Female Bolsheviks and women workers in 1917* (Terry Mayer)

Possible futures
L. Pantich and C. Leys (eds), *Necessary and Unnecessary Utopias: Socialist Register 2000* (Jason Edwards)

Editorial

As Matthew Worley points out in his contribution to the current issue, the definition of culture has aroused considerable theoretical debate. Nor are politics and political terms any less easy to pin down. Thankfully, the articles which follow do not get bogged down with such semantic problems, and their emphasis shifts between political culture and cultural politics without much deference to theoretical border controls. Instead, by engaging with the making of alternatives in a range of actual historical contexts, the contributors show how various were the interactions between creative activity and the world of politics, and how the politics of the left may itself be regarded as a form of creative activity.

The first two articles deal with issues of rupture and continuity in the British and French radical traditions. Andrew Whitehead's focus on a particular historical moment—the emergence of socialism in late Victorian Britain—and a particular locality, Clerkenwell, enables him to give a vivid sense of the sorts of issues and personalities on which these developments turned. Clerkenwell may not have been 'typical'—hence the epithet 'Red London', the title of a series of articles on the district dating from the 1870s—but the evidence here suggests that the emergence of a distinctive socialist politics represents a more significant moment of discontinuity than some recent accounts have allowed.

However, the case of London's 'Belleville' also offers much to suggest the resilience of older radical traditions. This emphasis on continuity is more especially the concern of Bernard Moss in his wide-ranging discussion of 'Socialism and the Republic in France'. Where socialists in Britain have tended to accentuate the break with nineteenth-century liberalism, in France a more insurgent republican tradition has been claimed by the left, and more specifically the communist left, as its own. In tracing this ideological inheritance, Moss shows how patterns of political allegiance established already in the early nineteenth century can be detected in support for the PCF even to the present day.

Two further articles take up more directly the relationship between the communist movement and culture. Judith Harrison and Liam O'Sullivan suggest that in the formative case of the Russian revolution this relationship was a distinctly uneasy one. Describing the emergence of a vibrant and subversive visual culture in early twentieth-century Russia, they note how initially these same artists embraced October as if it were the realisation of their own aspirations. Briefly perhaps it was: but while for some years a bold experimentation continued in fields such as film and architecture, it is argued here that already by the time of Lenin's death the plastic arts had been subordinated to the expediencies of the party.

'Keep culture out of Cambridge', wrote John Cornford at the tail-end of the Third Period, and at no time did the Communist Party in Britain display such hostility to bourgeois culture as during that of Class against Class. On the other hand, Matthew Worley argues, the CPGB succeeded at this time in creating a distinctly proletarian culture displayed with considerable effect in the workers' film, sports and theatre movements. Politically, this period has often been portrayed as a disaster. Matthew Worley would contest that argument, and the evidence he presents here is a reminder of the breadth of factors to be taken into account in reaching any considered verdict.

In the last of this issue's articles, Martin Wasserman draws attention to a neglected aspect of the life of Franz Kafka. In view of Kafka's reputation as anything but a mid-European Sidney Webb, his depiction by Wasserman as a key industrial reformer is not the least intriguing of the connections made here between politics and culture.

Among the reviews in this issue, John Saville contributes the first of a series of retrospective assessments of books deserving to be better remembered: in this case, *The Enormous Room* by e.e. cummings. There is also a review by Alison Ravetz of *Picture Windows* by Rosalyn Baxandall and Elizabeth Ewen, which readers will remember from the section adapted for *Socialist History* 16.

The next issue has as its theme 'life histories' and will feature contributions by Richard Pankhurst, Andy Croft and Alison Macleod, as well as an interview with John Saville by Malcolm Chase to commemorate the appearance of the tenth volume of the *Dictionary of Labour Biography*.

Socialist History Journal

The *Socialist History Journal* explores and assesses the past of the socialist movement and broader processes in relation to it, not only for the sake of historical understanding, but as an input and contribution to the movement's future development. The journal is not exclusive and welcomes argument and debate from all viewpoints.

Other *Socialist History* titles:

A Bourgeois Revolution?
Socialist History 1 · 1993
0 7453 08058

What Was Communism? Pt 1
Socialist History 2 · 1993
0 7453 08066

What Was Communism? Pt 2
Socialist History 3 · 1993
0 7453 08074

The Labour Party Since 1945
Socialist History 4 · 1994
0 7453 08082

The Left and Culture
Socialist History 5 · 1994
0 7453 08090

The Personal and the Political
Socialist History 6 · 1994
0 7453 08104

Fighting the Good Fight?
Socialist History 7 · 1995
0 7453 10613

Historiography and the British Marxist
Historians
Socialist History 8 · 1995
0 7453 08120

Labour Movements
Socialist History 9 · 1996
0 7453 08139

Revisions?
Socialist History 10 · 1996
0 7453 08147

The Cold War
Socialist History 11 · 1997
0 7453 12411

Nationalism and Communist
Party History
Socialist History 12 · 1997
0 7453 12675

Imperialism and Internationalism
Socialist History 13 · 1998
1 85489 1073

The Future of History
Socialist History 14 · 1998
1 85489 109X

Visions of the Future
Socialist History 15 · 1999
1 85489 1154

America and the Left
Socialist History 16 · 1999
1 85489 1170

International and Comparative Labour
History
Socialist History 17 · 1999
1 85489 1197

Red London
Radicals and socialists in late-Victorian Clerkenwell

Andrew Whitehead

Among the banners unfurled on Clerkenwell Green for a procession to Trafalgar Square in February 1867, when the Reform League's campaign for manhood suffrage was at its most tempestuous, were two bearing the slogans 'Put your trust in God, but keep your powder dry' and 'Disobedience to tyrants is a duty to God'. Fully twenty years later, with the temper of metropolitan radicalism once more rising and leavened by the emergence of militant socialism, another rally on Clerkenwell Green destined for Trafalgar Square (though it never got there, being stopped by police amid clashes which became known as Bloody Sunday) witnessed banners with these same uncompromising, yet somehow unmenacing, sentiments.[1]

This would appear to be telling evidence of continuity of tradition from the high point of mid-Victorian radicalism to the development of a distinctly socialist movement. London-wide and local studies of the Social Democratic Federation, the most important socialist organisation of the 1880s, have emphasised the extent to which it borrowed and developed from radical traditions, agenda and personnel. The most comprehensive study of working-class politics in late nineteenth-century London has suggested that the early SDF won support from the same kind of working men who formed the backbone of London radicalism, and that it was in the newer suburbs, where radicalism was less well established, that the socialist movement most easily took root. A study of Battersea in inner London, home to the most successful of the SDF's branches in its early years, has buttressed this argument by pin-pointing its strength in the newly built Shaftesbury estate, 'the acme of London working-class respectability', where again socialism was able to pick up on values and aspirations elsewhere promoted by radicalism.[2] The example of Clerkenwell, conspicuous in its contribution to mid-century radicalism and ultra-radicalism and the home of one of the biggest branches of the Social Democratic Federation in the 1880s, challenges this argument. Here the SDF built up its strength in the face of a powerful local radical tradition. While there was considerable co-operation between the two movements, there was little recruitment from one to the other, and still less in the way of a common local political agenda or form of organisation. Indeed, in its emphasis on the concerns of the unskilled and unorganised, the Clerkenwell SDF adopted a strategy quite distinct from that of the radical associations and clubs. The political dividend that this approach delivered was not long lasting. But the examination of the political ebb and flow in an area of London noted—some contemporaries would have said notorious—for the temper of its popular politics suggests a more complex and antagonistic relationship between Liberal radicalism and early socialism than has often been imagined.

In the debate about continuity between the popular radicalism of mid-century, the Liberal radicalism of later decades, and the emerging Labour and socialist movements, the evidence from Clerkenwell can be made to fit both sides of the argument.[3] In Clerkenwell, there was a continuous current of radicalism through the nineteenth century and into the socialist groups which flourished in the area. In terms of political tradition, a robustly assertive local radicalism fed into the development of explicitly socialist movements. Without the rich culture of radical clubs and secular societies, the lineage through Chartism and advanced radicalism, early socialist organisations in Clerkenwell would have been of much more feeble growth. Radicals and socialists mustered side-by-side on Clerkenwell Green and elsewhere to champion free speech, franchise reform, and fair play for Ireland. Yet however central these issues were to local radicalism, they were not the core of political activity for the Clerkenwell SDF. It addressed distinct issues largely overlooked by the local radical clubs, and found recruits from among those not previously prominent in local political organisations. The burst of political adrenalin which established the SDF as a local force suggests that it was seen by participants as something new, something exciting and different, rather than a reworking of old political nostrums. It was not a complete rupture from the past, not a repudiation of radicalism, but it was significantly different and a moment of discontinuity in the temper of popular politics.

London's Belleville

'We have no doubt in Clerkenwell our Belleville', one disapproving commentator declared in the aftermath of the Paris Commune.[4] The area's reputation for political militancy was in part a product of its central location. Clerkenwell was home to several meeting venues which at times gained notoriety. The Spenceans' insurrectionary meetings in the years after the Napoleonic wars were often held at Spafields, where Exmouth Market now stands. A short distance away was Coldbath Fields, where a police constable was stabbed to death during a reform meeting in 1833—the inquest jury decided it was a justifiable homicide.[5]

Clerkenwell Green, though neither verdant nor spacious, was the scene of some of the most heated of Chartist rallies in London in the 1840s, and again became prominent as an ultra-radical venue a generation later. In 1871, it was described by a journalist as 'the head-quarters of republicanism, revolution and ultra-nonconformity'.[6] In August of that year, the Metropolitan Police sent Gladstone a report on thirty-six potentially troublesome political meetings held in London between 1867 and 1870, of which twenty had taken place on Clerkenwell Green. Most of these meetings, Gladstone was informed, were organised 'by a small set of troublesome, and utterly disreputable agitators'.

> It would appear that no matter what is the ostensible subject selected by these men for their speeches, they invariably digress to abuse their betters; and this not in moderate or decent language…with scoundrels…who bawl themselves hoarse in denouncing the Queen in terms which [would] befit a brothel. The addresses delivered at the ordinary Sunday meetings at Clerkenwell appear to be invariably of this character. Indeed one cannot read these reports without wondering that such things dare to be uttered in any meeting of Englishmen.[7]

In later years, the early socialist movement made good use of the spot. H.M. Hyndman, the founder of the Social Democratic Federation, recalled with his all too customary condescension how:

> I first stripped myself of my class prejudices when I addressed a gathering largely made up of rather debauched-looking persons round the old pump at Clerkenwell Green. I laughed a little at myself standing there in the full rig-out of the well-to-do fashionable, holding forth to these manifest degenerates on the curse of capitalism and the glories of the coming time.[8]

The Clerkenwell Vestry, annoyed by the nuisance of the crowds and the notoriety of the Green, from time-to-time proposed to enclose the area with railings, but never managed to see any scheme through.

Yet there is real substance to the legend of Red Clerkenwell, beyond simply a few rallying points. In the mid-1860s, the Clerkenwell and Holborn branches of the Reform League were the most vigorous in London, and among the most radical, 'exhibiting an activity so energetic it almost rivalled the central Executive'.[9] The various ultra-radical groups which sprang from the Reform League were well represented in Clerkenwell, and one of these spawned the Patriotic Club on Clerkenwell Green, among the most renowned of London's radical working men's clubs.[10] Charles Bradlaugh's Hall of Science lay just east of Clerkenwell, and the area had several secularist and freethought societies. There was a powerful tradition of Liberal radicalism, which saw the return as the local Member of Parliament in 1892 of the first Indian to be elected to the House of Commons. And the Clerkenwell branch of the SDF was, in the formative years of the Federation, apparently second only to Battersea in size. There could be no better area to study the continuities and discontinuities between popular radicalism and early socialism.

Yet even Londoners could be forgiven, before the recent renaissance of the area at least, for asking—where is Clerkenwell? Clerkenwell long ago suffered administrative anonymity, being swallowed up into the Borough of Finsbury a century ago, which in turn became the most southerly part of the London Borough of Islington in the 1960s. The civil parish of Clerkenwell, the area under the care of the Clerkenwell Vestry in the late nineteenth century, stretched far beyond the immediate vicinity of Clerkenwell Green. It was an area of 315 acres, encompassing Pentonville, Sadlers Wells, the squares and circuses of Amwell, a fair part of what was Little Italy, and much of the former watchmaking area around Northampton Square, and extending south almost to Smithfield and the Barbican. At its peak in the 1881 census, the population was a little short of 70,000. It's always been an amorphous area with no centre, no commanding industry and a mixed social profile. By the 1860s, the wealthy had left Clerkenwell, their houses in the south of the parish had been subdivided, and the local élite consisted largely of small traders and business people. There were several large local landlords, who attracted the opprobrium of the Royal Commission on the Housing of the Working Classes of 1884–5 for their acquiescence in insanitary housing, but most played little role in the life of the area (though the house agents were a powerful force on the local Vestry). A generation later, the artisans were also leaving Clerkenwell—pushed out by the decline of the labour intensive crafts and trades with which the area had been associated, and by a vigorous programme of road building and slum clearances which tore the stuffing out of Victorian Clerkenwell. A local rector writing in the mid-1880s, looked back with a moist, but perceptive, eye on the demographic changes which had enveloped the area:

Within the time covered by Her Majesty's 'happy reign', merchants, lawyers, doctors, wealthy watchmakers and jewellers...lived in Red Lion Street and S. John's Square, and kept their carriages in the adjacent Mews. Early in the present reign a movement set in towards the suburbs. It was easy for such people to have their houses and gardens a few miles north-wards, at Highbury, Hampstead, or Highgate, and drive daily into business. Presently, the trades people followed their example. The houses thus emp-tied were let out in tenements, and were largely occupied by working jewellers, compositors, and printers...Now the Underground Railway has enabled many of these men to escape from the gloom of mid-London every evening, and to occupy the streets of houses which have been run-up—each house on its own tidy garden plot—in Tottenham and other Northern suburbs. Hence has arisen the anomaly that few of the work-ers in the Parish dwell in it, and few of the dwellers in it work in it.[11]

As if to bear out this account, one of the central characters in George Gissing's *The Nether World*, published in 1889 and the most commanding of the Clerkenwell novels of this era, moved out to Holloway and on to Crouch End while remaining in the employment of a die sinking works in Clerkenwell.

A brass plate on every door

Allied to the growing distance between residence and workplace in under-mining Clerkenwell's old political tradition, was a far-reaching change in the last years of the nineteenth century in the local economy. Clerkenwell had long been a bastion of the artisan, often working at home or in a small work-shop. It was an area, Gissing wrote in *The Nether World*, in which 'every alley is thronged with small industries; all but every door and window exhibits the advertisement of a craft that is carried on within....In Clerkenwell the demand is not so much for rude strength as for the cunning fingers and the contriving brain'. In the words of one of Charles Booth's researchers, Clerkenwell was still 'a two-storied parish, the houses have a respectable appearance and on nearly every front door is a brass-plate on which the occu-pation of the owner is proclaimed'.[12]

'Clerkenwell may be said to be the headquarters of the British watch trade', declared the trade's directory.[13] While the number of Clerkenwellians directly employed may never have exceeded a thousand, the horological trades helped define the local economy. In the last decades of the century, the trade was decimated by Swiss, French and American competition.

Clerkenwell remained loyal to traditional work practices involving an acute sub-division of labour, with not only watches but some of their parts passing through several workshops before they were fully assembled. The artisans of Clerkenwell refused to mechanise, or even standardise watch parts. The Booth survey interviews with watchmakers, conducted in 1893–4, read as a requiem for the trade. A Hatton Garden watch jewel dealer asserted that 'the London watch trade was dead and had ceased to be through its own fault', and the tale was told of 'one of the best [watch] dial painters [who] was now in the Shoreditch workhouse breaking his heart tying wood bundles'.[14] There was no significant tradition of labour organisation within the trade. Hermann Jung, a Swiss émigré who was one of the very few Clerkenwell watchmakers conspicuous in radical politics as secretary of the First International, wrote in 1868 that 'watchmakers keep aloof from anything akin to trade unionism. They have no connection with other trades; in fact they are quite ignorant of their doings'. More than twenty years later, the Booth survey echoed this point, commenting that 'the want of organisation is remarkable in London. There exists no union either among masters or men: and though there are now few employers of labour, yet the old tradition still survives'.[15]

If watchmaking contributed little to the tone of popular politics in Clerkenwell, the other defining local trades—jewellery and precious metals—were only slightly more conspicuous. Jewellers and goldsmiths weathered the end of century crisis besetting the artisan trades much better than the watchmakers, but had a fitful record of trade organisation and of political involvement. The local occupations more evident in moulding local politics were in the printing and paper trades. Clerkenwell's location just to the north of Fleet Street and Paternoster Row made it particularly suitable for printing businesses. There were large newspaper offices—the *Clerkenwell News* was to become the *Daily Chronicle*—as well as specialist printing houses, such as Gilbert and Rivington with its expertise in foreign and oriental type, and any number of small jobbing offices. There were also several bookbinding establishments, and some of the specialist sub-trades, such as book edge gilding, were almost a Clerkenwell monopoly. Other prominent local industries included some of the more specialist crafts within the furniture trade (John Betjeman's verse autobiography, *Summoned by Bells*, includes a description of the family's fancy cabinet making workshop in Pentonville) and small engineering and metal workshops. All of these were buffeted by the crisis in the inner London economy in the closing years of the century, and even in the industry least directly affected, printing, compositors were among the first to take advantage of the workmen's trains and to move out of central London.[16]

The larger industrial buildings flanking the newly built arterial roads bisecting Clerkenwell were mainly given over to warehouses and factory based production. Some of these workplaces were large, as evidenced by a local strike in 1889 said to have involved as many as 400 women envelope makers. The model dwellings also built along Farringdon Road and Rosebery Avenue would, by and large, have been unwelcoming to artisans, because of the local hostility towards their uniformity. (Gissing described one local model dwelling as 'terrible barracks…Vast, sheer walls, unbroken by even an attempt at ornament'), and the strict regulations against homeworking. The opportunities for casual labour were not as well developed as further east, and the larger docks were too far away to provide much work for Clerkenwellians. But the overall picture of Clerkenwell in the later nineteenth century is of an area where the local economy shifted from an emphasis on craft and skill to demand for semi-skilled and unskilled labour, with the remaining skilled and artisan workforce increasingly choosing to commute from the newly-built north London suburbs.

Between radicalism and socialism

Although the social and economic character of Clerkenwell was changing rapidly in the final third of the nineteenth century, and although the involvement of the local trades in political movements was very uneven, there is no doubt that local radical and socialist movements were dominated and led by skilled workers. There were some differences in social composition. Quite a few of the leading local socialists did not enjoy the job security normally associated with their trades, and the socialist organisations appealed for the active involvement of the less skilled in a way that the radicals did not. Yet the most striking contrast between radical and socialist groups was not in their composition but in their concerns. Radicals fought for an extension of the franchise, for secular and democratic education, and for working men Parliamentary candidates. In the wider political sphere—their outlook on Ireland and on foreign policy—radicals were motivated by a sense of morality, and of equity and fair play. And because radicals were a substantial force within local Liberalism, much of their energy was expended in factional battles and in contests over the selection of candidates. The early socialist movement, in contrast, adopted the issues not of the artisan but of the semi-skilled and unskilled, the issues of unemployment and new unionism. These were causes which had at times been championed by some of the ultra-radical groups, but were not regularly addressed—indeed were hardly addressed at all—by the main local radical institutions.

The persistence of radical movements in Clerkenwell was much commented upon by contemporaries. In the mid-1880s, the *Democrat* remarked upon what was still a vibrant political tradition:

> This district has long been regarded as the centre of London democracy. At any rate, the men of Clerkenwell have been the most active politicians of the extremist school, and their voices are always heard wherever the Radical flag is unfurled. They have ever shown a courage, a boldness, even an audacity, that are highly commendable, and which have done much to keep the Radical light burning when elsewhere it seemed likely to die out.[17]

The light burned most strongly during the Reform League agitation for the extension of the franchise in the mid-1860s. The League was of considerable importance in metropolitan, and indeed nationwide, radicalism because of the political breadth of its support base, and because its perceived success with the passage of the 1867 Reform Act gave an enormous impetus to radical movements. From its ranks sprang several of the leading local figures in mainstream radicalism over the next generation, and the founders of the more militant organisations which harboured a robust, declamatory and oppositional political tradition.

The energy and militancy of the Reform League branches in Clerkenwell and neighbouring Holborn was largely the contribution of a group of followers of Bronterre O'Brien, an Irish-born Chartist and land and currency reformer. The O'Brienites provided an element of continuity from the declining years of Chartism into the new radical movements. They became prominent in a range of organisations from the International Working Men's Association to the early Social Democratic Federation, as well as the Land and Labour League, the Manhood Suffrage League, and a remarkable but unsuccessful venture to establish a co-operative colony in Kansas. The O'Brienites' main base was in Soho, but they also had a strong influence in several other of what had been the artisan quarters of inner London, areas such as Clerkenwell and Marylebone.[18] The other main strand of continuity was the rationalist and secular movement, which pre-dated Chartism, subsisted alongside it, and survived as an organised force, to enjoy full bloom in the three decades from the mid-1860s. Secularism provided the broader radical movement with many of its leaders, most notably Charles Bradlaugh, but also much of its political agenda and its press.

One consequence of the success of the Reform League, and the increased political influence of artisans, was that Liberal party organisation in Clerkenwell became a forum for conflict between two traditions of radical-

ism—the old small employer and shopkeeper radicalism with which the
Finsbury constituency had long been associated, and the progressive radicalism of the skilled worker. The divisions between these two loosely defined
camps were intensified first by the redistribution measure accompanying the
1884 Reform Act, through which Clerkenwell (as Central Finsbury) became
a separate single-seat Parliamentary constituency, and then by the first elections to the London County Council in 1889. While there were political
disagreements—over education, Ireland and social issues—the most heated
and divisive debates were about democracy within the Liberal organisation
and above all about the selection of candidates. The split became so severe
that in 1886 a Conservative won what should have been the safe Liberal seat
of Central Finsbury, though by a majority of just five, and all—complained
the *Clerkenwell Chronicle*—'through the apathy and indifference of the
Radicals'. In the end, after much bitterness, the progressive radicals won
through. One of their favourites, F.A. Ford, was elected to represent the area
on the first LCC (though he came second to Earl Compton, another 'progressive' and the son of Clerkenwell's biggest landlord). Three years later,
Dadabhai Naoroji became the local Member of Parliament, though by
another single figure margin, so prompting some of his tongue-tied
Clerkenwell constituents to refer to him as Mr 'Narrow Majority'. One of
his committee rooms, and venue for a victory celebration, was the Patriotic
Club.[19]

The main reason why the local branches of the Reform League gained a
certain notoriety in the local and national press was their reputed sympathy
for the Fenians, the name given to supporters of the Irish Republican
Brotherhood. In particular, James Finlen of the Reform League's Holborn
branch was noted for his championing of the cause of Fenian prisoners
under sentence of death, and even led a sixty strong deputation of working
men to the Home Office, delivering an impassioned and threatening speech
immediately outside the Home Secretary's first-floor private office.[20] The
issue became much more emotive after the 'Clerkenwell outrage' of
December 1867 when several local people were killed by a powerful bomb
explosion outside the walls of the local jail, in an unsuccessful attempt to
enable the escape of a leading figure in the Irish Republican Brotherhood.[21]
Finlen was hounded by the press over his political sympathies and the alleged
neglect of his children to such an extent that subscriptions were raised to
fund his passage to America, though he eventually settled, under an assumed
name, in Lancashire.[22]

The intriguing issue is the extent of not simply political sympathy, but
clandestine collaboration, between Fenianism and groups within the Reform

League. The League's leadership was enormously sensitive to charges of collusion with the Irish Republican Brotherhood, though such substantial figures within the League as George Odger and Charles Bradlaugh made clear their understanding not simply for the Fenians' goal, but for the temper of their agitation as well. After the Clerkenwell explosion, and the popular revulsion to which it gave rise, the most prominent radicals distanced themselves from the Fenian movement. But prior to that, there is evidence of contact and co-operation between the IRB and sections of the Reform League. An informer confided to police officers investigating the Clerkenwell bombing that:

> I have been told for a positive fact, by a man named Barratt, that the Reform League had a 'revolution society' formed amongst themselves, & were in communication with Col. Kelly.[23]

General Cluseret, a veteran of the American Civil War and other military campaigns who became commanding officer of the Fenians in Ireland, recalled that he had 'a nocturnal meeting with members of the Executive Committee' of the Reform League, and that later 'the basis of an agreement between Fenianism and the Reform League was agreed upon'. There is another account of such contacts from a senior, and disapproving, figure within the Reform League.[24] Whatever the extent of these links, the Metropolitan Police was sufficiently alarmed to step-up surveillance on local branches of the Reform League, and indeed to put pressure on pub landlords to refuse to let their rooms for meetings. This petty harassment of local radical groups persisted for several years. And when the police sought to close down a discussion group which had developed from the Holborn branch of the Reform League—meeting at a beer house with a suitably conspiratorial name, the 'Hole-in-the-Wall'—money was raised from radical worthies, and in July 1872, the Patriotic Club opened on its own leasehold premises on Clerkenwell Green.[25] It remained there for twenty years, through the decline of ultra-radicalism and the emergence of a local socialist movement, and throughout that time was one of the most prominent participants in the radical working men's club movement in London.

The Patriotic Club

The Patriotic Club, as with so many of London's radical clubs, mixed a radical agenda—in favour of Home Rule for Ireland and a Republic for the rest of the British Isles—with those equally important aspects of club life, recreation and alcohol. The club had a lecture room and a library, and also bagatelle and billiard tables and a bar. 'Those who know the place and its chiefs', complained a correspondent to the *International Herald*, 'know that it is a rum-selling concern in which politics are regarded from a pecuniary point of view'.[26]

Local radicals tended to predominate in the Patriotic's lecture list, but speakers on literature and adventure were also popular, and the O'Brienites' influence within one of the main lecturing organisations, the Social and Political Education League, ensured that their views were well heard. The core of the Club's political activity was its sponsorship of radical causes and organisations, the holding of open-air meetings on the Green, and the large contingents paraded on demonstrations and processions through central London. The Club was a stalwart of the Metropolitan Radical Federation and of Republican organisations. When E. Douglas Jerrold wrote a series of articles on 'Red London', the Patriotic Club featured prominently.[27] Yet its lectures and debates only occasionally touched on local issues, such as the poverty and unemployment among the casualised workers of inner London so evident just a short stroll from the Club. It rallied to the support of striking agricultural labourers, but rarely expressed solidarity with the semi-skilled and unskilled labour on its doorstep.

There's no authoritative figure for the membership of the Patriotic Club, but it is possible to give some account of its social composition. For a few years, the Club became a limited company, and so was required to submit company records which are now deposited at the Public Record Office.[28] The signatories of the 1875 Memorandum of Association illustrate the range of membership: a fixture dealer, a trimming seller, an engraver, an engineer, a plumber, a porter, a plasterer, two tailors and a printer. A broader picture of Club membership can be gleaned from the lists of shareholders, a rare insight into the social profile of London radicalism, though the shareholders may not have been entirely representative of the Club membership. In 1880, the Club had 139 shareholders, each with one share. All were men, and this in spite of a decision immediately prior to the Club's foundation that women should be eligible for membership. Almost all the shareholders lived within walking distance of Clerkenwell Green, demonstrating that although the Patriotic had a London-wide reputation, its catchment area was local. A dozen of the shareholders were shopkeepers, dealers or travellers, another half dozen were clerical workers, and a further twelve were in unskilled jobs. The remainder, almost four-fifths of the total, were skilled workers. The horological trades accounted for just five shareholders, and workers in precious metals for another ten. Fifteen workers in engineering or base metals were listed, along with twenty building workers of various types (including as many as seven plasterers), and twenty-three workers in the printing and paper trades, among them thirteen printers or compositors and seven bookbinders. Some of the shareholders would no doubt have worked for themselves or been workshop proprietors, others might have wished to support the Club because of its social activities rather than its political reputation, nevertheless these records are a powerful reaffirmation of the dominant role of skilled workers in Clerkenwell radicalism.

The precise political character of the Patriotic was fluid. The O'Brienites who were so important in its foundation lost sway after a few years. The Club kept some distance from mainstream Liberalism, and on occasions sponsored radical candidates to challenge Liberal MPs. 'There's the Patriotic', declared the *Radical* in 1882, 'that has certainly shaken off the yoke of the Liberal party, and now has the courage to act for itself'.[29] However, it still came within the tradition of Liberal radicalism, and when in the 1880s a correspondent from a radical paper visited the Club he noted that the walls were lined with portraits and photographs of Gladstone, Dilke, and other Liberal leaders, albeit of a radical hue. The Patriotic's early membership of the Democratic Federation (the precursor of the SDF), and the plethora of socialist speakers at the Club, cannot be taken to imply any strong socialist sympathy among the membership. The local branch of the Socialist League appears to have been decidedly optimistic in declaring that 'there are several Socialists members of the club, and a prospect of winning more over to the cause'. A more telling comment may perhaps be that of an old-time socialist who recalled how the radicals at the Patriotic used to lean out of the Club windows and heckle the SDF speakers on Clerkenwell Green.[30]

The Tichborne claimant

If the Patriotic Club was one radical Clerkenwell institution which, through its longevity, provided a link between the heyday of local radicalism and the early socialist movement, another—less conspicuous, but equally robust in its radicalism—was the local support network for the Tichborne claimant. The Magna Charta Association was formed to protest the rights of an apparently ordinary working man—Arthur Orton to his detractors, but Sir Roger Tichborne to the Magna Chartists—who claimed heirdom to a large estate. The claimant and his court cases were the main cause of the Association and its paper, the *Englishman*, but its full programme, while idiosyncratic, was notably progressive, adopting some of the points of the old Charter and taking a particularly advanced line on what was then known as 'the woman question'.

The Tichborne movement has been described as 'one of the largest (if not the largest) popular movements between the end of Chartism and the development of socialism and independent Labour politics in the 1880s and 1890s'.[31] It was derided by some prominent radicals as frivolous and worthless, but the Tichborne case caught the popular imagination, became a celebrated cause intertwining issues of equity and social justice, and attracted into popular politics many who might not otherwise have aligned themselves with radical and democratic movements. When the Magna Charta Association adopted a branch structure in 1875, five branches were founded in the Finsbury area, of which two survived for more than a decade. The contrasting strands of the Association's policies were reflected in the branch banners. Islington's banner read 'We advocate Triennial Parliaments and the release of Tichborne', while Clerkenwell's, paying tribute to the Association's founder, bore the legend, 'Three cheers for Dr. Kenealy and the Republic'. The Tichbornites interested themselves in local issues, and in 1878 they led a successful campaign against one of the Clerkenwell Vestry's plans to 'enclose' Clerkenwell Green. The Association was prone to internal feuding, and began to lose momentum after the death of Dr. Kenealy in 1880. In the years to the Association's final disintegration in 1886, Clerkenwell was one of its few remaining areas of strength. The branch supported Home Rule and anti-coercion protests, heard a number of socialist speakers, and was briefly an active constituent of the Democratic Federation. Jack Williams, who was for a time a local officer of the Magna Charta Association, was in 1883-4 the secretary of the Clerkenwell branch of the Democratic Federation and became one of the best-known members of the SDF.[32] Along with what remained of the O'Brienites and the small English section of the Social Democratic Club, the Association's branches were among the few radical groups antipathetic to Liberalism, and that hostility was in part bequeathed to the local SDF.

Establishing the SDF

The Social Democratic Federation has been tainted by the idiosyncrasies of its founder, H.M. Hyndman, and its perceived allegiance to political concepts which restricted its ability to engage with newly emerging forms of trade unionism. The notion of a dinosaur-like SDF, shackled by the prejudices of its leader and by an inflexible adherence to concepts such as the 'iron law of wages', persists in spite of local studies which suggest that SDF branches were not impeded in involving themselves in labour disputes and in new unionism.[33] The history of the Clerkenwell SDF certainly emphasises that whatever the party line, branches were able to pursue a healthy political pragmatism about which issues they pursued and which campaigns they made a priority. Clerkenwell was one of only three branches of the SDF which were continuously in existence from 1884 to 1902—the others being Battersea and Blackburn.[34] The Federation's local lineage dates back even earlier. The 'No. 1' branch of the Democratic Federation met regularly at the Crown Tavern on Clerkenwell Green at the close of 1881. Two years later, Clerkenwell and Marylebone were the only branches to hire halls to continue lecture programmes over the winter. The Clerkenwell SDF—the name of the organisation changed in 1884, though the adoption of a socialist programme came the previous year—became firmly established in the winter of 1884, by addressing an issue on which local radicals rarely campaigned: unemployment, and the need for public works programmes. The Social Democratic Federation first turned to unemployment as a campaign issue during the closing weeks of 1884, on the initiative of a former officer in the Royal Artillery, H.H. Champion, and his schoolmate at Marlborough, Percy Frost. It was something of a travelling circus, moving from one 'centre of agitation' to another, with the unabashed aim of helping a new organisation, and its still newer branches, win attention and recruits. 'Champion and Frost ...sketched out a good plan of campaign for London this winter', William Morris confided in September 1884.[35] The following month, George Bernard Shaw went further:

> But for Frost and Champion, who, though nominally Hyndmanites, practically boss the Federation between them by sticking together and working (they have kicked up a flourishing agitation in the East End) the whole body would have gone to pieces long ago.[36]

The agitation started in Limehouse in November, but after a few weeks the SDF paper, *Justice*, recorded that it was time 'to move the agitation to the district of Clerkenwell, in order that the Clerkenwell branch which has recently been formed and which has already done active work may be strengthened'. In the New Year, the campaign moved on to Bermondsey, but by then its purpose had been served in Clerkenwell. Meetings were held nightly for two weeks, not just on Clerkenwell Green but at half-a-dozen other locations in Clerkenwell and neighbouring St Luke's. It was the sort of propaganda blitz that radical groups no longer even attempted.

Although not really a local figure, Henry Hyde Champion, who had been much influenced by the writings of the land reformer Henry George, took the Clerkenwell branch under his wing. He was an energetic and domineering young man, who had resigned his army commission in the autumn of 1882, and put much of his money in a progressive publishing enterprise, the Modern Press. He won the confidence of Hyndman—both had privileged upbringings, a sympathy for Empire and a distrust of Liberal radicalism—and became the Federation's secretary and one of its most prominent figures before breaking with the SDF and becoming an early and important advocate of independent labour representation. His appetite for intrigue, questionable sources of finance and imperious personality eventually made him something of an outcast in the British labour movement, and he emigrated to Australia in the early 1890s.[37]

As well as kick-starting the agitation on unemployment, Champion also found the Clerkenwell branch a meeting place, an old lodging house, apparently with an unsavoury reputation, in Hatton Wall. It had a large room for lectures and meetings, which became known as the Phoenix Hall, and was a considerable asset to the branch. The hall was used not only for lectures and branch meetings, but for SDF annual conferences, concerts and dances, and social evenings in aid of Federation funds. One of these gatherings was a tea and concert, held on 5 July 1886, to mark the inauguration of an SDF Club on the premises. More than a hundred people attended. It was the fourth London SDF branch to obtain permanent premises. Here, as elsewhere (and in marked contrast to the Patriotic Club) there was no alcohol, something in which the SDF took considerable pride.[38] The wife (or perhaps mother) of a branch member provided Sunday dinners 'for men only' at 'prices to suit all pockets'—the only reference found to women's involvement in the Clerkenwell SDF during the 1880s (though one branch member suggested 'singing some good Socialist songs' at meetings to try to 'win the women into our ranks who, up to the present, have to some extent been an unapproachable section'). An advertisement in *Justice* indicated the range of activities planned for the Club:

Phoenix Club, Hatton Wall, Clerkenwell.—The above Club is now open to any member of the Federation on payment of twopence per week…Classes will be held for French, English, Debating, Drilling and Shorthand. The games include Bagatelle, Chess, Draughts, Cards, Athletics, etc. Entertainment will consist of Concerts, Dances, Lectures, Social Gatherings, etc.

The 'drilling' mentioned so casually in the advert was no idle threat, and was sufficient to excite the fears of the Metropolitan Police which had been keeping an eye on the SDF ever since the West End Riots a few months earlier.[39]

Champion had reportedly advised a meeting of the unemployed, in the over-heated rhetoric common in the early years of the SDF, to join the Volunteers, learn how to drill and get a rifle. In September, the Commissioner, Sir Charles Warren, reported that Clerkenwell was among three SDF venues in which drilling was taking place. Within a few weeks, the drilling had stopped, apparently without overt police intervention. But Sir Charles Warren remained sufficiently anxious to submit to the Home Office in the New Year one of Champion's signed editorials in *Justice*, which argued that force should only be used as a last resort, but

> should the blindness of our rulers ever drive the people to such desperate courses I trust there will be many among the English revolutionists who will have the wit to see that as soon as an appeal to force becomes inevitable, the swifter and heavier the blow struck, the better in the long run for the side that takes the initiative.[40]

The attractions offered at the Phoenix Club—from Sunday lunch to military-style parading—were reflected in the membership of the Clerkenwell SDF. At its relaunch in November 1884, it had fifteen members, and subsequent fluctuations can be traced, albeit hazily, through the branch subscriptions forwarded to headquarters and acknowledged in *Justice*.[41] Throughout 1885, branch membership hovered about the twenty-five mark. Then in the late summer of 1886, at around the time of the opening of the Club (and when the SDF was attracting considerable local attention), membership rose rapidly, reaching around 120 in the spring of the following year. Over this brief period, Clerkenwell was apparently the Federation's second biggest branch after Battersea—though it was never able to emulate the success of the Battersea branch in local government—and accounted for up to a fifth of the total dues paying membership, which at this time was almost exclusively in London. The closure of the Phoenix Club in June 1887—coinciding with the expulsion from the branch of a prominent Irish activist, the limiting of the branch catchment area with the creation of a new Islington branch, and H.H. Champion's increasingly public breach with the SDF—pushed membership down to about forty, a figure not exceeded over the next decade. The Clerkenwell SDF never regained its early membership or energy and gradually declined into a political torpor.

Marshalling the unemployed

The issue of the unemployed, which the Clerkenwell SDF had used to good effect in getting itself established, was addressed with still greater vigour at the beginning of 1886. The Federation had been badly bruised a few weeks earlier by what became known as the 'Tory Gold' scandal, when it was revealed that the SDF had accepted money from Conservative sources to help finance dismally unsuccessful candidates in the 1885 general election (and, so the Tories hoped, split the radical vote). 'The Federation are convicted of offering to sell their fictitious numbers to the highest bidder (in money, not in reforms)', George Bernard Shaw declared to a political colleague. 'All England is satisfied that we are a paltry handful of blackguards'.[42] The revelation badly damaged morale, and still more importantly, made Liberal radicals deeply suspicious of the SDF and so damaged the links built between the SDF, the breakaway Socialist League and some of London's radical clubs, notably at free speech demonstrations to preserve an outdoor speaking pitch at Dod Street in Limehouse. The authorised historians of the SDF declared that after the scandal, 'it was decided to put every ounce of effort into the agitation on behalf of the unemployed'.[43]

It was this campaign which brought the SDF to national attention. The issue was well chosen. In the mid-1880s, an acute cyclical depression caused widespread unemployment and hardship, at just the time that the economic base of inner London was changing from old-established handicraft industries to an economy based on casual and unskilled labour. In the winter of 1885–6, and the two succeeding winters, there was acute distress in working-class districts of London, and much higher than usual seasonal unemployment. In the spring of 1887, the government sought to quantify the extent of the unemployment problem and enumerators questioned some 30,000 working men in four districts of London.[44] Clerkenwell was not one of the areas chosen, but the findings would have been as applicable here as elsewhere. More than half of those questioned said they had been unemployed at some time in the previous five months, and more than a quarter were unemployed at the time of asking.

The Clerkenwell branch of the SDF initiated the revival of the unemployed agitation. It organised meetings of those out-of-work, and bombarded the local MPs, the Board of Works and the Board of Guardians with demands for publicly financed projects on which the unemployed could work and for an easing of restrictions on relief for those not admitted to Workhouses. The SDF became established as the main lobbyist for the unemployed. A columnist in the radical *Clerkenwell Chronicle* was obliged to state that 'my friends the Socialists are up and doing good work, I hope, in their endeavour to relieve the sufferings of their distressed fellow working men', while a correspondent to the paper said that although he could not support the full objectives of the SDF, the work of the local branch on behalf of the unemployed was to be commended.[45] H.M. Hyndman, the founder of the SDF, trumpeted that there was 'no doubt whatever that the agitation on behalf of the tens of thousands of unemployed workers in London so vigorously begun by the Clerkenwell branch…and taken up with equal earnestness and energy by the Marylebone and St Pancras, the Battersea, the Hackney and Shoreditch, and the Limehouse branches will develope [sic] into a really formidable movement'.[46]

The temper of this agitation can be gauged from the speeches made at a meeting of the unemployed at Holborn Town Hall, called by the Clerkenwell SDF, on 3rd February 1886. Champion chaired the rally, and Hyndman delivered an emotive address, describing himself as a 'Revolutionary Social Democrat':

> They must put the fear of man in the hearts of their opponents. The Social-Democratic Federation did not intend to lead the men up a hill to take them back again. There was many a man in this room whose life was not worth living under present conditions. Was it not better for them to die a sudden death than to be crushed into a pauper's grave by destitution. (Applause).

Later in the evening, the SDF's John Burns said that 'as an unemployed workman he felt that it was infinitely preferable to die fighting than to die starving'. This was fighting talk—and five days later, the fighting started, with the much chronicled disturbances in central London which became known as the West End Riots.[47] The violence, and the subsequent trial and acquittal of four SDF leaders—Champion, Hyndman, Burns and Jack Williams—was marvellous publicity for the Federation. It wasn't quite sure how to respond. 'We do not care for our lives', H.H. Champion declared in the aftermath of the trouble, with typical bravado, 'and when you find a body of resolute men who are perfectly willing to die in defence of their cause, you may depend upon it this trouble will not soon be overpast'.[48] The SDF maintained this insurrectionary tone for a few months, but in the longer term, the effect of the rioting and its aftermath was to promote a more cautious political style.

The increasing awareness of the plight of the unemployed, and the alarm created by minor rioting in central London, prompted a surge in charitable donations. In Clerkenwell, local clergy set up their own relief fund, while the Holborn Board of Guardians followed the example of the Clerkenwell Vestry in establishing a special committee on the unemployed question. The

Board also opened a stone-breaking yard in Golden Lane in St Luke's. One of the Guardians was horrified by what he heard on a visit to the yard:

> He saw [those working in the yard] that afternoon and he could say that out of the twenty-six in the yard there were not five of them worthy of being taken from the stone-breaking. They said if the Guardians did not deal as they thought right with them they would join the Social Democratic Federation.[49]

The following week, there were eighty men in the stone yard, and the Board was obliged to introduce wood chopping to make sure there was enough work for all those seeking out-relief.

While the unemployed agitation was making an impact on local government and the churches, it seems to have left Clerkenwell's radical groups unmoved. At this time, an internecine feud within the local Liberal and Radical Association was at its height. Ward meetings were being held to effect the Association's reorganisation, and the bad feeling within the liberal and radical camp was intense. As for the Patriotic Club, it was busy converting its hall into a 'bijou theatre'. The member of the Board of Guardians most sympathetic to the unemployed movement—Samuel Brighty, a longstanding radical, veteran of the Reform League and an officer of the Patriotic Club in its early years—was rewarded by being swept off the Board in local elections early the following year. The Clerkenwell SDF, however, persisted with its campaign, kept it going through the politically lean summer months, and returned to it with some vigour in the winter, when seasonal unemployment made the issue much more pressing. The branch organised canvasses of the unemployed, demonstrations, church parades, and even offered cooked breakfasts to the children of the unemployed on Sunday mornings, attracting as many as 200 waifs who were obliged to sing 'The Marseillaise' as a form of grace.

There were increasing divisions within the SDF, both locally and among the national leadership, about political tactics. H.H. Champion and Tom Mann were increasingly arguing for a campaign to seek legislation to reduce the hours of labour and an emphasis of Labour representation in Parliament, while others wanted a more militant, and less reformist, tone. By the beginning of 1887, there was a strong feeling among some of the SDF's leaders than the unemployed agitation had ceased to bring dividends. Few of the unemployed became members, there was little tangible success in instigating public works, and the campaign was draining morale. Hyndman described it as a 'long, weary and depressing agitation'.[50] By the time of the first anniversary of the West End Riots, the SDF was not as proud of its role in the disturbances as it had been in the immediate aftermath. It did not welcome the initiative of the Clerkenwell and Marylebone branches in holding an evening rally on Clerkenwell Green and torchlight procession to mark the anniversary. The Metropolitan Police banned the procession, and orders were given to break up any march. Nevertheless, a small crowd assembled, and there were some disturbances before the demonstrators were dispersed. The SDF executive sternly disapproved of the episode, and Ernest Belfort Bax told William Morris that the Clerkenwell and Marylebone branches came close to expulsion.[51]

In another indication of its independent spirit, the Clerkenwell SDF persisted in its agitation among the unemployed to a greater extent than most other London branches. In the autumn, it once again started hounding the local establishment, prompting one member of the Clerkenwell Vestry, a Liberal, to comment 'he believed that the officials of the Social Democratic Federation were charlatans of the worst type, still he must admit they were doing a little good'.[52] The unemployed agitation gained a tempo of its own in the autumn of 1887, with gatherings of the unemployed on Clerkenwell Green and Trafalgar Square.[53] In time, a committee was formed out of these assemblies, the Unemployed Registration Committee, which brought together members of the SDF and the Socialist League. The Federation's leadership appears to have been annoyed by the involvement of the Clerkenwell SDF, and the branch secretary felt it necessary to write to *Justice* to state 'it is true that some of the Committee are members of the Clerkenwell branch…but they are acting entirely independent of the branch in every sense'. A year later, regular meetings of the unemployed were again held on Clerkenwell Green, but with less vigour. The Federation's annual report for 1889 recorded that 'as regards the unemployed agitation, the SDF has not been so active this year as in other years. The reason for this has been the unemployed agitation requires some fresh method of working'. It was only in the mid-1890s that the SDF returned to the unemployed issue.

New unionism

Another issue had emerged, however, to absorb the attention of London's socialists—an issue which again involved organising those with little tradition of political involvement and which served to distinguish the SDF from the radical clubs and groups. The wave of new unionism did not break like a cloud of thunder when the Bryant and May match girls went on strike in 1888. Unions such as the Alliance Cabinetmakers' Association had been seeking to organise the less craft-based sections of the artisan trades for the previous twenty years. But at the close of the 1880s, there was a series of strikes—the match girls, then the gas workers and above all the London dockers, all of them by-and-large successful—which prompted the formation of a rash of new trade unions, many of them short lived, recruiting among workers with no history of labour organisation

The SDF's commitment to new unionism has been questioned by some historians of British Marxism, who have suggested that the Federation was encumbered by a distrust of labour organisation and reservations about the effectiveness of industrial action.[54] This argument asserts that the unemployed movement of 1886–7 was the biggest mass movement in which the early SDF was involved, and suggests that if consolidated by a more vigorous involvement in new unionism, it could have established the Federation as a considerable force within the labour movement. There is certainly an issue to be addressed: the failure of the SDF in London to expand after its initial burst of growth. The SDF's dues paying membership for 1887 was not exceeded on a national level until 1892 and the considerable growth in the mid-1890s was due to its success outside London, and particularly in Lancashire. But while the evidence of the Clerkenwell SDF confirms that little energy was expended in organising within existing trade unions, there seems to have been no reluctance in promoting the creation of new unions.

The first reference to the Clerkenwell SDF's encouragement of new trades unions dates from February 1887, when the United Society of Shop Assistants gave its address as the SDF Club in Hatton Wall. The branch gathered modest amounts of money to support the striking dock workers in 1889. More importantly, it played a key role in a subsequent strike of printers' labourers, being the dominant force on the strike committee, which met at the branch's new venue, a coffee house on Clerkenwell Green. The strike was largely successful, and the strike committee began to take the form of a Printers' Labourers' Union, which was the direct predecessor of the National Society of Printers and Assistants (NATSOPA), one of the main print unions through most of the twentieth century.[55]

George Walden, the member of the Clerkenwell branch most involved in the printers' labourers dispute, seems to have had an almost missionary zeal for establishing new unions. He organised the Printers' Warehousemen, Cutters and Paper Trade Union, and a Metropolitan Police Union. Other branch members established a Shop Assistants, Warehousemen's and Porters Union. The SDF's failure to grow in London towards the end of the 1880s cannot simply be ascribed to an ambivalence towards trades unions and strike action. Yet the Clerkenwell branch didn't grow as a result of its attempts to organise the semi-skilled and unskilled. Just as the unemployed agitation did not bring any great number of the out-of-work into the Federation, the foundation of new unions also failed to bring in many recruits.

Who were the SDF?

The inability of the Clerkenwell SDF to find, or at least keep, recruits from among the unemployed and the newly organised raises the question: just who did join the local branch? There are no records extant to provide a full answer, not even the equivalent of the Patriotic Club's lists of shareholders. What can be stated with certainty is that Henry Hyde Champion, the ex-artillery officer turned socialist propagandist, was quite untypical of the branch. Of the three branch secretaries of the Clerkenwell SDF in the 1880s, the occupation of the first is unknown, the second was a compositor, and the third a carpenter. Yet, in the last two cases, these simple descriptions of their occupation conceal a chequered employment record. The compositor was a self-employed job printer. And the carpenter, William Bowman, appears to have made only a precarious living from his trade. He received substantial unemployment benefit from his union, and in October 1887, a 'benefit concert' was held to raise money for him as he had 'the misfortune to be laid up, with his children, with fever. Comrade Bowman has had very little work for the last eighteen months, which makes his position more severe'.[56] George Walden, the champion of new unionism, was among other branch members sufficiently impecunious to require an appeal for financial help.

In all, the occupations have been established of fourteen of the members of the Clerkenwell branch in the second half of the 1880s—three compositors, two carpenters, two bricklayers, an electrical engineer, a shop assistant, a silver engraver, a confectioner, a shop blind maker, a labourer and a publisher (this being the least inaccurate occupational pigeon-hole for H.H. Champion). It seems that the leading members of the branch were largely skilled workers, though not in what would have been regarded as the archetypal Clerkenwell trades, and often not enjoying the status and income associated with skill. In some ways, the branch appears to have straddled the divide between the old artisan Clerkenwell and the new more casualised local economy, without being firmly embedded in either. This perhaps partly explains the impression gained by Frank Galton, an engraver and later an associate of the Webbs, when he and a friend came across the Clerkenwell SDF:

We discovered a branch of the SDF meeting behind a poor coffee shop on Clerkenwell Green and we both joined there. But...we found the members a poor lot, there was little or no propaganda, and in fact it seemed to be a sort of gathering of down and outs to discuss their grievances rather than a serious group for the discussion of socialism. So we very soon left.[57]

His judgement seems harsh, given the apparent energy of the Clerkenwell SDF, but it's likely that many members' association with the branch was similarly fleeting.

Whatever the institutional continuities between some branches of radicalism and the early socialist movement, there is little evidence that the Clerkenwell SDF won its recruits from within the radical movement. Of the twenty-eight people identified with tolerable certainty as members of the Clerkenwell branch over the period 1884–90, only one had previously achieved even minor prominence within local radicalism—George Bateman, a printer and ex-soldier who went on to be a colleague of Champion on the *Labour Elector*, who was threatened with expulsion by the Holborn Liberal and Radical Club because of his socialist sympathies. It is remarkable that the Clerkenwell SDF organised in the face of a powerful radical tradition, without apparently winning over to its cause any of the important, or indeed second rank, figures in local radicalism. For instance, of the 139 shareholders in the Patriotic Club in 1880, not one is known subsequently to have joined the Clerkenwell branch of the SDF.[58]

The temper of the branch was, however, decidedly militant. The Clerkenwell SDF appears to have had a reputation for a robust, even hot headed, approach to political issues. One account of a socialist demonstration in Trafalgar Square in November 1886 gave a flavour of this. 'It is said that there are now from 120 to 140 Social Democratic 'lodges' in London', the *Penny Illustrated Paper* reported, with some exaggeration:

Chief among them is the Clerkenwell branch. 'They're red-'ot members, they are,' ejaculated an admiring Socialist as the men of Clerkenwell took up their position. These had two blood-red banners, surrounded by the *bonet-rouge* of the French Revolution.[59]

The French Revolution appears to have been something of an inspiration to the branch. One member of the Clerkenwell SDF wrote an angry letter to a local paper to repudiate accusations by a member of the Holborn Board of Guardians, Mr Leaver, that the unemployed made their plight worse by lack of thrift:

Mr Leaver has doubtless read of a gentleman who, when the people of Paris asked them [sic] for bread, told them to eat grass. Soon after that gentleman was found hanging from. a lamp-post, with some of the stuff he had advised other people to eat rammed into his mouth. I should recommend Mr Leaver to profit by his example, because there are grass plots and lamp-posts in London.[60]

The letter may not have left Mr Leaver trembling, but it does point to an uncompromising political tone. That's seen even more clearly in an unpublished letter of March 1885 from a member of the Clerkenwell SDF to the editor of the Socialist League's paper, *Commonweal*, soliciting support for a campaign to persuade the Local Government Board to establish public works. 'This once got it will be the begining [sic] of a great Social reverlution [sic]', he declared, 'which can end in one way only namely the compleat [sic] Emancipation of the working Class'.[61] This messianic sense of the imminence of a socialist society was very much part and parcel of the early SDF, and that's why it's misleading to equate the Federation's championing of palliatives, or 'stepping stones' as they were sometimes called, with a moderate, temperate reformism.

The anarchists

The almost millenarian tone of some Clerkenwell socialists, along with their belief in the revolutionary potential of the outcast and a robust indifference to Parliamentary action, suggests a political approach which has much in common with anarchism. There was, indeed, a strong anarchist current within the early SDF, and particularly among several of those active in or on the fringes of the Clerkenwell branch.

The strength of anarchist sentiment within William Morris's Socialist League has been much more extensively documented than similar sympathies within the Social Democratic Federation. When the League broke away from the SDF at the end of 1884, one of the main points of contention was the expulsion of members with alleged anarchist sympathies, though the overriding issue was Hyndman's autocratic style of leadership. In Clerkenwell, the branch secretary of the SDF, E.J. Baxter, went over to the League, but he is the only seceder who has been identified. Some of the SDF branches under William Morris's sway in west London, and the Labour Emancipation League in the East End, went over more or less in their entirety to the League, but otherwise it seems that few London rank-and-file members changed allegiances. The Socialist League had an active group in Clerkenwell, which briefly published its own newsletter, the *Labor Leaf* (later revived as the *Anarchist Labour Leaf*). Relations with the local SDF appear to have been good, though the Socialist League was conspicuously less active in the unemployed and new unionism movements, and was much the smaller in terms of local membership and profile.

Yet the reservoir of support for anarchism within the local Social Democratic Federation—and not just for anti-statist sentiments but for an explicitly anarchist outlook—was considerable, even after the breakaway of the Socialist League. In the early years of the SDF, anarchism was an important element within the socialist movement and had adherents within the Federation. It was only in 1890 that conference voted not to allow anarchists to remain within the SDF, and in spite of this decision, anarchist sympathies endured within the Federation in the early 1890s. It has been suggested that SDF members who were themselves in casualised occupations and subject to unemployment were more involved in militant campaigns and more sympathetic to anarchist ideas.[62]

The first issue of *Justice* in January 1884 reported that the Federation's founder, H.M. Hyndman, was to give a lecture to the Clerkenwell branch on 'Socialism v Anarchism'. He again addressed the branch on this same issue almost two years later in December 1885. On this latter occasion, he was responding to a lecture given the previous week by Charlotte Wilson, (whose four part article on 'Anarchism' had been published in *Justice* and who in 1886 was a founding editor of the anarchist journal *Freedom*), entitled 'Anarchism and Social-Democracy'. The report of her talk in *Justice* stated that the 'long and interesting' discussion which followed her lecture 'showed that the disagreements between the lecturer and her audience were not so grave as might be supposed'. Those may not simply have been the polished words of an excessively polite branch secretary, for the Phoenix Social Democratic Club, the shortlived Club established by the Clerkenwell SDF, appears to have been the place were several of those later prominent in the anarchist movement in London got to know each other.[63] And two members of the Clerkenwell SDF in the late 1880s, Tom Pearson and Charles Morton, went on to be longstanding members of the Freedom Group.

The event which contributed more than any other to the growth of the anarchist movement in London in the 1880s was the execution in November 1887 of four anarchists, the 'Chicago martyrs', for allegedly throwing a bomb at police dispersing a public meeting. The SDF, the Socialist League and the Freedom Group were all active in the campaign for clemency for those under sentence of death. In mid-October, the Clerkenwell branch of the SDF, having heard a lecture on the Coming Revolution from its branch secretary, the unemployed William Bowman, unanimously passed a resolution 'against the judicial murder of the Chicago Anarchists'. At this time, the more-or-less spontaneous gatherings of the unemployed in Trafalgar Square were gaining strength. Two days after the hangings in Chicago came the violence of 'Bloody Sunday', when the Metropolitan Police clashed with London socialists and radicals trying to enter Trafalgar Square to stage a demonstration linked to the movement against coercion in Ireland. The writer J.H. Mackay in his documentary novel *The Anarchists* captures in dramatic fashion the political impact of this close sequence of events. Anarchism became a powerful force within the admittedly restricted confines of the London left. In June 1888, the Clerkenwell SDF held a debate, advertised as open only to Federation members, on 'Is Anarchism immediately practicable?' Tom Pearson spoke in support of the proposition. He was active both in the SDF and in the Freedom Group, and the following summer he established a North London Anarchist Communist group meeting in Islington. Also in the summer of 1889, the Patriotic Club hosted a debate, organised by the Clerkenwell branch of the Socialist League, on the relative merits of Social Democracy and Anarchist Communism, which was long remembered as one of the highlights of left-wing politics of this period.

There was a steady haemorrhage of SDF members to the Freedom Group and other Anarchist groups, which persisted, at a much slower pace, into the 1890s. The visit to London at the end of 1888 of Lucy Parsons, the widow of one of the Chicago martyrs, signalled something of a turning-point, as her espousal of violence repulsed many in the SDF. The increasing association of anarchism in continental Europe with 'propagandism by the deed', with assassination and outrage, also served to isolate London anarchists from other socialists.[64]

The peddling of rudimentary anarchist and insurrectionary ideas by local propagandists such as Dan Chatterton, at one time a committee member at the Patriotic Club and later a regular attender at SDF and Freedom Group meetings, must also have increased awareness of such notions.[65] The gradual eclipse of anarchist ideas within socialist groups, and the growing antagonism between anarchists and Marxists, should not be allowed to conceal the attraction. of anarchist ideas in the late 1880s, particularly in Clerkenwell and one or two other areas of inner London.

Red London?

Clerkenwell's reputation for political militancy persisted into the twentieth century, but in much attenuated form. The old tradition of artisan radicalism died out with the artisan trades themselves in the closing years of the nineteenth century. The increasing dislocation between residence and work-place further eroded the political traditions which had once been so strong in the Clerkenwell area. It's intriguing that two militant socialists brought up in Clerkenwell whose political coming of age fell in the early years of the new century, Tommy Jackson and Guy Aldred, both emphasise in their auto-biographies the importance to their political development of the artisan radical milieu in which they grew up.[66] Yet the early socialist movement which was at one time so strong in Clerkenwell owed only a modest amount to the area's radical lineage.

It has to be supposed that the area's rich radical pedigree encouraged an independence of spirit, and discouraged a deferential or quiescent approach to political and religious matters. But in Clerkenwell, much more than in other early SDF strongholds in London, the socialist movement developed not because of local radicalism, but in spite of it. There was virtually no direct recruitment to the SDF from the main local radical organisations. The two movements co-operated, usually happily, on issues of common concern, and marched side-by-side to dozens of central London demonstrations. But in the tone of their politics, Clerkenwell's radicals and socialists had little in common. The Clerkenwell SDF sought to address the concerns of the new Clerkenwellians, those in irregular employment and in unorganised indus-tries, concerns which were largely ignored by the 'old Clerkenwell' radicals. In terms of building up a political organisation, the dividends for the local SDF, and for the political tradition it represented, were decidedly modest. Yet in one of the few areas which spanned the divide between mid-Victorian radicalism and the socialism of the closing years of the century, the socialists were not simply an old radicalism in new guise, but marked a more considerable discontinuity in political style and agenda than has often been appreciated.

Notes

1. *Clerkenwell News*, 12 Feb 1867. Donald C. Richter, *Riotous Victorians* (Athens, Ohio, 1981), p.144. This article is based on research conducted for my uncom-pleted University of Warwick doctoral thesis, 'Popular Politics and Society in Clerkenwell, 1865–1890'. Draft chapters of the thesis can be consulted at the Finsbury Library, 245 St John Street, London EC1 and at the Marx Memorial Library, 37a Clerkenwell Green, London EC1. I am grateful to Professor Tony Mason for his encouraging comments on an earlier version of this article.
2. Paul Thompson, *Socialists, Liberals and Labour: the struggle for London, 1885–1914* (London, 1967), pp.115–16. Janet McCalman, 'Respectability and working-class politics in late-Victorian London', *Historical Studies*, 19, 74, 1980, pp.108–24.

3. The most cogent exposition of the continuity thesis is the introductory essay in Eugenio F. Biagini and Alastair J. Reid (eds), *Currents of Radicalism, 1850–1914* (Cambridge, 1991), pp.1–19. A more nuanced version is presented in Rohan McWilliam, *Popular Politics in Nineteenth-Century England* (London, 1998), pp.67–80.
4. *Morning Post*, cited in Andrew Rothstein, *A House on Clerkenwell Green* (London, 1966), p.39,
5. Gavin Thurston, *The Clerkenwell Riot: the killing of Constable Culley* (London, 1967).
6. *City Press*, 2 September 1871.
7. Gladstone Papers, British Museum Add MSS 44617, ff.95–105.
8. Henry Mayers Hyndman, *The Record of an Adventurous Life* (London, 1911), p.341.
9. A.D. Bell, 'The Reform League from its origins to the Reform Act of 1867' (Oxford, D.Phil., 1961), p.167.
10. The story of the building which housed the Patriotic Club, now the Marx Memorial Library, is recounted in Rothstein, *Clerkenwell Green*.
11. Rev. William Dawson, *A mid-London Parish* (London, 1885), pp.40–4.
12. British Library of Political and Economic Science (BLPES), Booth Manuscripts, A 10, f.35.
13. *Kelly's Directory of the Watch and Clock Trades* (1880 edition), p.iv.
14. Booth Manuscripts, B 90, ff.11–12, 32–3.
15. *Beehive*, 17 October 1868. Booth Manuscripts, A 10, f.35.
16. The decline of London's 'inner industrial perimeter', marked by the relocation of those industries which remained viable and the shrinking of those tied to the inner city, is discussed in Gareth Stedman Jones, *Outcast London: a study in the relationship between classes in Victorian society* (Oxford, 1971).
17. *Democrat*, 27 December 1884.
18. For the O'Brienites, see Alfred Plummer, *Bronterre: a political biography of Bronterre O'Brien, 1804–1864* (London, 1971); Royden Harrison, *Before the Socialists: studies in labour and politics, 1861–81* (London, 1965), pp.210–50; Stan Shipley, *Club Life and Socialism in Mid-Victorian London* (Oxford, 1971); Watson Eugene Lincoln Jr, 'Popular radicalism and the beginnings of the new socialist movement in Britain, 1870–1885' (London, PhD., 1977); Andrew Whitehead, 'The New World and the O'Brienite colony in Kansas', *Society for the Study of Labour History Bulletin*, vol. 53, no. 3, 1988, pp.40–3; Mark Bevir, 'The British Social Democratic Federation, 1880–1885: from O'Brienism to Marxism', *International Review of Social History*, 37, 1992, pp.207–29.
19. The most recent of several biographies of Dadabhai Naoroji is Omar Ralph, *Naoroji, the first Asian MP* (Antigua, 1997). The story of his nickname is recited in a pamphlet, *Memories of Finsbury 1880–1900, by old residents* (London, 1955), p.9. Rothstein, *Clerkenwell Green*, p.51.
20. PRO HO 45/7799, 1310–17. See also James Finlen, *Mr J Finlen's defence of himself against the attacks made upon him by the Parliament and Press of England* (1868).
21. For the Clerkenwell explosion, its antecedents and ramifications, see Patrick Quinlivan and Paul Rose, *The Fenians in England, 1865–1872* (London, 1982).

Quite the most remarkable aspect of this incident is the failure of the police to prevent the explosion, even though Home Office and Metropolitan Police papers at the PRO demonstrate that they knew an escape attempt was imminent and how it would be carried out, and that an unsuccessful attempt to blow up the prison walls was made (the rescuers could not get the fuse to light) a day before the actual explosion.

22. The *Beehive*, 25 September 1869, reported a meeting at the Hall of Science 'to hear a farewell address from Mr Finlen previous to his departure for America'. George Howell, however, came across him twenty years later, living in poverty in the Warrington area—Manuscript autobiography of George Howell, vol. d, f. 37, Howell papers, Bishopsgate Institute.

23. PRO MEPO 3/1788, statement by Patrick Mullaney, 19 January 1868. Colonel Thomas Kelly was the senior figure in the Irish Republican Brotherhood.

24. General Cluseret, 'My Connection with Fenianism', *Fraser's Magazine*, July 1872, pp.31–46. John Bedford Leno, *The Aftermath* (London, 1892), pp.71–2. Charles Bradlaugh, although disapproving of Fenian tactics, helped write the Fenian Proclamation of 1867, and was in touch with both General Cluseret and Colonel Kelly: see Hypatia Bradlaugh Bonner, *Charles Bradlaugh, a record of his life* (London, 1894), vol. 1, p.253. The issue of radical sympathies for Fenianism is discussed in John Newsinger, *Fenianism in mid-Victorian Britain* (London, 1994), pp.47–65.

25. *National Reformer*, 7 July 1872. Rothstein, *Clerkenwell Green*, pp.41–2. Lawrence Marlow, 'London's Working Men's Clubs: some aspects of their history, 1860–90' (Warwick, MA, 1972), p.15.

26. *International Herald*, 18 January 1873. For other descriptions of the Patriotic Club, see *Radical*, December 1887, *Clerkenwell Chronicle*, 30 January 1886, and Andrew Rothstein, 'Radical clubs in the eighties', *Quarterly Bulletin of the Marx Memorial Library*, 90, 1979, pp.7–9.

27. The article in this series on the Patriotic Club appeared in the *Weekly Dispatch*, 6 July 1879.

28. PRO BT31, 2079/9248.

29. *Radical*, 3 June 1882.

30. *Labor Leaf*, September 1886. Rothstein, *Clerkenwell Green*, p.55.

31. Rohan McWilliam, 'Radicalism and popular culture: the Tichborne case and the politics of 'fair play', 1867–1886', in Biagini and Reid, *Currents of Radicalism*, pp. 44–64.

32. *How I Became a Socialist* (London, 1896), pp.37–8. H.W. Lee and E. Archbold, *Social Democracy in Britain* (London, 1931), p.86. John Saville, 'The background to the revival of socialism in England', *Bulletin of the Society for the Study of Labour History*, no. 11, 1965, pp.13–19.

33. The argument for a politically sclerotic SDF is put most cogently in Henry Collins, 'The Marxism of the Social Democratic Federation', in A. Briggs and J. Saville (eds), *Essays in Labour History, 1886–1923* (London, 1971), pp.47–69. A more measured account can be found in Martin Crick, *The History of the Social-*

Democratic Federation (Keele, 1994).

34. I am indebted to Paul Watmough for this information.

35. Morris to Andreas Scheu, 28 September 1884, International Institute for Social History, Amsterdam (IISH).

36. Shaw to Scheu, 26 October 1884, cited in Henry Pelling, *The Origins of the Labour Party, 1880–1900* (London, 1965 edn), p.29.

37. I am grateful to Professor John Barnes for his kindness in showing me a draft of his forthcoming and enormously revealing biography of Champion.

38. *Justice*, 26 June 1886, commented about the opening of a Social Democratic Club by the Paddington and Bayswater branch: 'Social-Democrats are showing here, as in Clerkenwell and Battersea, that working men can keep up Revolutionary Clubs without beer'. The Rules of the Phoenix Club, along with a list of office bearers, survive in the Friendly Society records at the PRO, FS3/270, 5305.

39. *Justice*, 11 September 1886. Victor Bailey, 'The Dangerous Classes in late-Victorian England' (Warwick, PhD., 1975), p.241. PRO HO144/183, A45225.

40. 'Mobs and Revolutions', *Justice*, 15 January 1887. This was Champion's lasted signed editorial for *Justice*.

41. For the methodology of estimating branch membership, see P. A. Watmough, 'The membership of the SDF, 1885–1902', *Bulletin of the Society for the Study of Labour History*, no. 34, 1977, pp.35–41. For its shortcomings see Crick, *History of the SDF*, pp.61–2

42. Shaw to Andreas Scheu, 17 December 1885 (IISH).

43. Lee and Archbold, *Social-Democracy*, p.109.

44. 'Tabulation of the statements made by men living in certain selected districts of London in March 1887', Parliamentary Papers 1887, vol. LXXI. M.J. Cullen, 'The 1887 survey of the London working-class', *International Review of Social History*, 20, 1975, pp.48–62.

45. *Clerkenwell Chronicle*, 6 February 1886.

46. *Justice*, 6 February 1886.

47. *Justice*, 6 February 1886. Richter, *Riotous Victorians*, pp.103–32.

48. 'From the Social Democrat point of view', *Pall Mall Gazette*, 9 February 1886.

49. *Clerkenwell Chronicle*, 20 February 1886

50. Hyndman, *Record*, p.370.

51. PRO H0144/B862. Florence Boos, 'William Morris's socialist diary', *History Workshop Journal*, 13, 1982, pp.30–2.

52. *Clerkenwell Chronicle*, 15 October 1887

53. There is a compelling account of one of these largely spontaneous gatherings of the unemployed in J.H. Mackay, *The Anarchists* (Boston, MA, 1891), pp.56–68.

54. Notably Henry Collins, 'Marxism'; also E.J. Hobsbawm, *Labouring Men* (London, 1968 edn), pp.231–8.

55. *Justice*, 31 August 1889; *Commonweal*, 21 September 1889. J. Moran, *NATSOPA: seventy-five years* (London, 1964), pp.12–21.

56. *Justice*, 23 October 1887.

57. F.W. Galton, manuscript autobiography (BLPES).

58. The shareholders list did make mention, however, of a certain Thomas Mann, described as a carpenter of 20 St Johns Lane. It is not clear whether this was the renowned socialist Tom Mann.

59. *Penny Illustrated Paper*, 27 November 1886, contained in a bound volume at the British Library entitled 'Socialistic Items Newspaper Cuttings 1886–8'.

60. *Clerkenwell Chronicle*, 8 May 1886

61. Socialist League archives, 2424 (IISH).

62. This point is made by Bob Baldwin in two unpublished papers, 'Constitutionalism or Revolution? Street politics and the socialist debate on strategy in late nineteenth century London' and 'Anarchists and Social Democrats in late nineteenth century London'.

63. Guy A. Aldred, *Dogmas Discarded* (Glasgow, 1940), vol. 2, p.60.

64. Haia Shpayer has argued that 'the practice of keeping a safe distance from the anarchists which had started in the late 1880s became entrenched in the 1890s, and ran parallel with the consolidation of the violent image of anarchism. The effect of this image on the progress of anarchism was crushing'; Shpayer, 'British Anarchism, 1881–1914: reality and appearance' (London PhD., 1981), p.185.

65. For the remarkable Dan Chatterton, see Andrew Whitehead, 'Dan Chatterton and his 'Atheistic Communistic Scorcher'', *History Workshop Journal*, 25, 1988, pp.83–99.

66. T.A. Jackson, *Solo Trumpet* (London, 1953), pp.34–43. Guy A. Aldred, *No Traitor's Gait* (Glasgow, 1955–63), part 2, pp.29–37.

Socialism and the Republic in France
A long view

Bernard H. Moss

In his inaugural declaration before parliament in June 1997 the French prime minister Lionel Jospin invoked the Jacobin ethos of civic morality against the corrupting spirit of individualism and money in public life to justify a new republican pact for the defence of education, jobs and the public sector.[1] The wagging tongues of the establishment daily *Le Monde* saw in this return to 'the republican model' the product of a deal with the new minister of interior Jean-Pierre Chevènement, leader of *Le Mouvement des citoyens*, a ginger group of republican socialists that was hardly in a position to dictate the terms of Jospin's political programme. Ignored by *Le Monde*, eternal apostle of the third way, was the deep entrenchment of the French left in the republican experience.

It was Jean Jaurès, the great historian and synthesiser of French socialism, who first stressed its dependence upon 1789 and 1792. For Jaurès, whose synthesis erred on the side of idealism, the French Revolution contained the whole of socialism, which was merely the principle of equality applied to property and pushed to its logical conclusion. To triumph over royal, church and aristocratic resistance the bourgeoisie had to appeal to the common people on the basis of a social democracy that asserted the rights of the nation to dispose of property.[2]

Socialist historians, even the factional representatives who collaborated on his *Histoire socialiste*, failed to develop his insight.[3] Like Marx they tended to regard their movement not as an outgrowth of republicanism, but as the result of an ideological rupture with that past.[4] Traces of the putative rupture between petty-bourgeois republicanism and working-class socialism can be found even in the best histories of the left by Maurice Agulhon and in the *Histoire de la France contemporaine, 1789-1980*, an otherwise fine multi-volume survey written by communist historians that sold as well as the anti-communist François Furet's in France but which is virtually unknown in Britain and the US.[5]

Conservatives since Edmund Burke have better understood the subversive potential of 1789 and 1792. From observation of the early days of the Revolution, Burke apprehended the threat that the philosophy of equal rights and the irruption of the masses posed to social order, hierarchy and property.[6] Returning to his Irish roots, he invoked traditional Catholicism to defend against the dangers of revolution. Tocqueville, like his latter-day successor Furet, blamed the Revolution for infusing the spirit of class struggle into modern politics. Fighting the totalitarian menace in 1952, Jacob Talmon found 'a living and unbroken tradition' of political messianism from Rousseau and Robespierre to Babeuf and modern socialists. What conservatives missed in this 'unbroken tradition' was of course the actuality of social conflict and the absolute centrality of the property question.[7]

The continuities between French republicanism and socialism and communism are profound—ideological, programmatic, geographic, religious and social.[8] The French left has always been both one and pluralist, often divided into multiple factions, but more or less united in aim and philosophy. The basic division was not between a statist or centralist and federalist or *autogestionnaire* culture, as Michel Rocard of the 'second left' claimed at the 1977 Socialist Congress of Nantes, but rather between a moderate wing appealing largely to the middle classes that was normally ready to compromise with the established order and a more consistent revolutionary wing entrenched in the working class. As in the process known as 'transformismo' in Italy, socialist deputies were often drawn by constituency pressures and the desire for office and minimal reforms into the moderate camp, causing a revolutionary backlash in the rank and file. This two-way movement had its geographical dimension in the retention by revolutionaries of the traditional bastions and the retreat of moderate representatives to the lukewarm periphery.

The French left has always been both centralist and *autogestionnaire*. The Jacobin clubs of 1793–94 were both a distinctive manifestation of local democracy and a movement of solidarity with the national cause; until 1794 Parisian clubs acted in conjunction with the *sans culottes*, the grassroots movement of shopkeepers, artisans and workers.[9] Through the trades assembly of the Luxembourg Commission the republicans of 1848 encouraged the parallel formation of federated trade societies and their democratically managed cooperatives. The Paris Commune of 1871 conjoined grassroots neighbourhood and trade democracy with central direction and co-ordination. The Jaurèsian synthesis in the Socialist Party combined parliamentary socialism with the direct action of syndicalism while the communists never completely abandoned the ideal of worker control in their plans for enterprise committees and tripartite management of the public sector.

The underlying aim was always the social or collective ownership and control of industry and protection of agriculture. The ideological thrust for public intervention in the market came from Rousseau and Robespierre's definition of property as a convention subject to the general will. The touchstone of republican socialism was a plan for the transformation after the democratic revolution of private enterprise into state-assisted union co-operatives run by workers. From that republican programme to the syndicalist vision of an economy arising from the violent overthrow of employers owned and operated by trade unions, which was also upheld by the early *Parti ouvrier* or workers' party, was only a small step taken as a result of the experience of the Commune and disenchantment with the conservatism of the new republic.[10]

Marx and Engels, who learned their politics from French republicans, thought the latter were 'communists without knowing it'.[11] In March 1848, before returning to Germany, Marx participated alongside Auguste Blanqui in the French club movement of 1848 hoping that the arming of the workers would keep the republican government moving in a socialist direction. His abandonment of 'petty-bourgeois' parliamentary republicans in favour of an insurrectionary workers' party was premature in 1849, but it prefigured the future of socialist politics and the Soviet revolution. Revolutionary, egalitarian, collectivist, and proletarian in the populist sense—everything disposed republicans toward the eventual embrace of Marxian socialism.[12]

The strength and durability of the left had its source in the alliance forged by the Jacobins between the working people of cities and towns and the emancipated peasantry, largely small-holding, found especially in the South and Centre of France. This alliance was revived by the democratic-socialists of 1849, the socialists of the 1890s and the communists of the Popular Front. What makes for French exceptionalism compared to Britain or Germany is less the statist tradition due really to Napoléon than the unending struggle, at first hidden and obscure, later broad and open, between democracy, understood as a coalition of middle and popular classes, and the forces of economic exploitation, social hierarchy and authoritarian rule.[13]

It is a dialectical history of social polarisation, radicalisation and repression that was inaugurated from 1789 to 1814, repeated in more extended form from 1830 to 1871, adumbrated in the Boulanger and Dreyfus affairs, and revived in the Popular Front and its Vichy revenge, a cycle that perhaps only really ended paradoxically with the student Revolutionspiel of May-June 1968, which by challenging communist hegemony on the left opened the way for the expression of a rejuvenated middle-class individualism in the 1970s and 1980s.[14]

Permanent revolution in France

Republicans in mid-century understood their movement to be a continuation of the great Revolution of 1789 in a process called permanent revolution in which the bourgeois revolution against king, church and aristocracy spilled over into social democracy and socialism. As Marx, who had analysed the constellation of social and political forces in Germany in 1843 as restoration *en permanence*, explained it, the French revolution was permanent in the sense that it was continuous, uninterrupted, and never stabilised, following an ascendant line of radicalisation and deepening of popular participation. To overcome the resistance of the old order, the more conservative bourgeoisie had to lean on more radical factions and rural and urban populace. As soon as more conservative factions from liberal monarchists to Girondists had brought the revolution far enough to be unable to follow it further, they were thrust aside by the bolder allies and eventually the Jacobins and Robespierre came to rule. But Robespierre and the *sans culottes*, with the threats they posed to the accumulation of wealth, were too much for most of the middle classes to bear, and they were executed and eliminated, not without a last-minute spasm from the poorer wage-earning section of the *sans culottes* who supported the communist plot of Babeuf.[15]

Marx and the republicans saw a continuation of this process in 1848 with middle-class moderates leaning on the working class to overthrow the July Monarchy. Frightened by the socialist aspirations thereby unleashed, the bourgeoisie retreated, suppressing the workers' uprising of June 1848 and calling upon a strongman named Napoléon to restore order. This left more radical republicans like Alexandre Ledru-Rollin to lead workers and peasants forward in the parliamentary elections of May 1849 until they came to grief in the confused and abortive uprising of 13 June. Reflecting on the break-up of the bourgeois-democratic coalition in Germany and the French defeats of June 1848 and 1849, Marx counted on a breakaway of revolutionary workers, under the leadership of Blanqui, from petty-bourgeois republican parliamentarians. This estimate was premature for 1849, but it prefigured the creation of workers' parties, not only in France, after 1880.[16]

The history of the left starts, not to the left of the president in the Constituent Assembly of August 1789, but in the split between two sets of middle-class lawyers in 1792, the newly-enriched Girondists, speaking especially for the merchant class of Bordeaux, and the Jacobins, who were willing to violate the newly won freedom of commerce to win over the support of working people for the Revolution.[17] The idiom that justified their choice, common to all groups in 1789, but more authentically felt and understood by the Jacobins, was that of Rousseau whose ideal of a levelling democracy of small holders they perceived in the movement of the *sans culottes*.[18]

To insist on the petty-bourgeois nature of this vision, as did Albert Soboul, is to forget the interventionist and levelling tendency of Jacobin rule and Robespierre's definition of property as a social convention subordinate to the prior right of existence. As Filippo Buonarroti, the companion of Babeuf, who passed on the memory of the conspiracy of the equals to nineteenth-century republicans, maintained, Robespierrism could and did lead on to communism.[19] While Robespierre defended private property in his lifetime, his Rousseauistic logic and worker allies, once abandoned by the bourgeoisie after his execution, moved in the direction of Babeuf's communism.

With ramifications in the army, the government and much of urban France, the conspiracy was, as recent work has suggested, larger and more significant than has previously been thought.[20] It specifically targeted though with uncertain success the poorer half of the Parisian population who were wage-earners and who had been left hungry, destitute and abandoned politically by the Jacobins after Robespierre's demise. The conspiracy was not an idiosyncratic spasm alien to the spirit of 1792, but its very expansion toward a more proletarian audience and collective ideals.

When the working-class movement revived in the revolution of 1830 after decades of Napoleonic and Restoration repression, it took a distinctly socialist direction. Republicans had since 1825 expanded their understanding of the Revolution with the help of Saint-Simonian conceptions of class and exploitation. The young Blanqui, who first tried to rouse the workers in 1827, already saw history as a series of class struggles leading to a transitional dictatorship and a co-operative commonwealth.[21]

The key organisation in this period was the Society of the Rights of Man and of the Citizen, which has never been seriously studied since Georges Weill explored social republicanism in 1900.[22] Possibly established on the traces of Jacobin clubs, which became increasingly artisanal in composition under the Directory, it emerged from popular disenchantment with the economic liberalism of the July Monarchy as exclusively working class.[23] It had at least 3000 members and 162 neighbourhood sections in Paris and claimed 300 affiliates in the provinces with traces in the North, West, Allier, Cher, Burgundy, the Jura, Rouen, Lyons, Saint-Etienne, Toulon and Toulouse and at least twelve known sections in towns and villages in l'Hérault.[24]

The sections were designed for both political education and insurrection, mixing workers with petty bourgeois and composed in Paris of worker sections led centrally by students and intellectuals. Their Robespierrist credo was a theoretical invitation to socialism and the programme they developed for state-assisted union co-operatives, later publicised by Louis Blanc, became the touchstone for republican socialism. The best testimony we have of this alliance of students and workers is from *Les Misérables* by Victor Hugo, who was an eye-witness to the first republican uprising in 1832 at the Cloître St-Merri.[25]

Much confusion has been sown by calling these workers artisans. Independent producers rarely strike. It is true that the *canuts* or silk weavers of Lyons, who occupied the city in 1831 and rose again in 1834, owned their own looms and employed helpers, but under competitive conditions they earned less than average wages and formed a concentrated rebellious mass in the city. In any event the strike movement of 1833 included all sections of the working class stirred by republican propaganda, mostly skilled workers but also mill-hands in adjoining towns and agricultural labourers in the Midi.[26] It was in response to this agitation that factory owners in rural areas began to introduce paternalist measures of welfare and clerical education that served to insulate a large part of the industrial working class from socialism.[27]

Suppressed after the second Lyons rebellion in 1834, the workers' movement went underground and took the form of the tightly organised secret society of Blanqui and others. During the electoral reform agitation of 1840 these secret societies took on the appellation 'communist', but they remained an integral part of the republican movement, the street-fighting vanguard of middle-class socialists like Ledru-Rollin who published the newspaper *La Réforme*. It was from these republican workers that the young Marx, arriving in Paris in 1843 with his head full of Rousseau's *Social Contract* and Robespierrist histories of the Revolution, discovered communism. Much ink has been spilt in an elusive purist quest lamenting the late or incomplete arrival of Marxism in France, but the fact is that French republicans were Marxians long before Marx.[28]

The revolution of 1848 was a repetition of 1792 with workers in the lead and co-operative socialism on the agenda.[29] More than 1789 it structured modern French politics. As in 1792 the initial strength of Republicanism was that it split the opposing propertied classes. Having witnessed the irruption of the masses in the Revolution, the Liberals of the July Monarchy had empowered only the wealthiest, the surest guarantors of order, protecting their landed, commercial and industrial monopolies. Other industrialists, merchants and professionals supported the moderate republicans, who advocated competition and free trade, but who in conflict with the Party of Order in 1849 were thrust to the side of the working class and republican social-ism.[30] One outcome was the emergence of a progressive republican bourgeoisie that, at least until the Clemenceau government of 1906–09 clashed with the unions, concerned itself with reconciling the working class by means of social reforms and a liberal co-operative socialism.[31]

The other strength of republicanism was the worker-peasant alliance. Most peasants owned land, but almost four-fifths of holdings, paying under 20 francs tax annually, were small, under ten hectares; their owners often depended on renting more land and wage earning.[32] The majority of peasants were land-hungry, burdened with debt and as resentful of landlords and creditors as they were fearful of the return of the old seigneurs. In terms of class they were as proletarianized small-holders in a comparable position to the *canuts* of Lyons. Where they were tied to urban villages by market relations or habitation and free from clerical domination, they were easily drawn to red republicans. Where republicanism was strong it also mobilised sharecroppers and rural labourers.[33]

Starting in September 1848 republicans reached out to peasants with a programme of easy credit, progressive tax and price support. In the election of May 1849 a third of the countryside, especially in the Midi, Southeast, East, and northern, western and south-western slopes of the Massif Central, voted red. Peasants formed the bulk of violent resistance to Louis Napoléon's coup d'état of December 1851. The French left—radical-socialists, socialists and communists—never ceased to defend the small-holding peasantry, who returned the compliment.[34]

The next great manifestation of republican socialism was the Paris Commune, which Marx saw as an incipient model for proletarian revolution. The experience of the Commune belies Rocard's theory of the two cultures, for it sought communal autonomy within a unified France, combining the grassroots democracy of neighbourhood and trade committees with the central co-ordination of a Committee of Public Safety approved in principle if not in name by virtually all Communards. Those working-class leaders who had been attracted to anti-statist Proudhonism in the early 1860s violated all its taboos against strikes, political action and collectivism once they had re-organised unions and joined with Marx and Bakunin in the First International.[35] As Martin Johnson has recently shown, Jacobins, Blanquists and internationalists worked together in neighbourhood clubs and city-wide federations acting as a virtual revolutionary party driving the communal revolution.[36] The signs, symbols and heroes of 1792 and co-operative programme of 1848 merged easily with the grassroots socialism of the international.[37]

Socialism, syndicalism and communism

The Third Republic did not, as Furet and many others have imagined, completely end the revolutionary cycle. Its constitutional laws of 1875 that gave veto power to a rural-oriented Senate were the result of a temporary deal, which republicans planned to revise, between Lèon Gambetta and the Orleanist oligarchy to avert the danger of civil war.[38] Its early affairs around General Boulanger and Captain Dreyfus, which divided France between republican and conservative blocs, were marks of social distress and constitutional discord.[39] In both affairs socialist workers played a leading, albeit unheralded, role in defending democracy against the threat of authoritarian rule. While middle-class republicans tended to accept parliamentary and capitalist horizons, the working-class element continued to pursue a revolutionary transformation.

If unions meeting at the third national labour congress in 1879 suddenly embraced revolution and decided to form a separate workers' party, it was because they believed the Republic consolidated in that year was pregnant with socialism. The strikes that burst out in the 1880s to celebrate and hasten emancipation had, as described by Michelle Perrot, the air of 1793 about them.[40] The widely reported defenestration of the engineer Watrin by the striking miners of Decazeville with whom the troops of Boulanger came to share their soup was a token of revolutionary expectations.

While defending the new republic against the danger of Caesarism, militants of the *Parti ouvrier* sanctioned leaders who sought too close collaboration with socially reformist republicans. The *Parti ouvrier* was split into anarchist, Marxist, Possibilist or reformist and Allemanist factions to which was added the older republican Blanquists. In the absence of a single revolutionary party at a time when first successes in the 1890s created electoralist illusions, trade unionists began to look to the general strike to bring about their 1789. Union backlash against the class-collaborationist overtures of the first socialist minister, Alexandre Millerand, produced the doctrine and movement known as revolutionary syndicalism, which embraced a majority of trade unions. Yet, even the scenario for the general strike written by anarchist leaders of the CGT, the union confederation, Emile Pouget and Emile Pataud, bore an uncanny resemblance to 1789.[41]

The leaders of the Socialists Jaurès and Edouard Vaillant came from the two traditional wings of republicanism, parliamentary and insurrectionary. As Jolyon Howorth demonstrated, Vaillant was never a disciplined Blanquist, but a republican intellectual who had passed through the school of Proudhon to join Blanquists and Internationalists in the Paris Commune later to find exile in London as Marx's closest ally.[42] Vaillant, less doctrinaire than Jules Guesde, the officially annointed Marxist, and less eclectic than Jaurès, exemplified the process by which republicans could become Marxists; after all the *Manifesto*, which was his primer, was written for a group of German workers steeped in the French revolutionary tradition. Unlike traditional Blanquists, who supported Boulanger as a nationalist who sought revision of the constitution, Vaillant defended the republic because he saw it securing the only free society in which the class struggle could be fought to its conclusion.

Jaurès was correct in his *Histoire socialiste* to see socialism emerging from republicanism as the result of a historical process. As an Opportunist deputy before 1890, he still naively believed that the republican party as a whole would become socialist.[43] There was some basis for this belief. As a recent study of the progressive bourgeoisie shows, but for the Senate, the new Republic would have passed perhaps the most advanced labour reforms, especially regarding union rights, in the world.[44] The Dreyfusard government and Millerand enacted a ten-hour bill that applied to both women and men working with them and they regulated working conditions in the semi-public sector and private firms operating under public contract. For many years, until Clemenceau's confrontation with syndicalism in 1906, unions achieved strike success only with the benevolent mediation of republican prefects and ministers.[45]

French syndicalism is often supposed to represent an incarnation of Rocard's 'second left' if not that of the irrationalist philosophy of Georges Sorel.[46] In fact, French syndicalism was the result of an organisational accident, the fragmentation of the *Parti ouvrier*, which made it impossible for any one political faction to control the unions. The strategy of the general strike was popularised by Allemanists in revolt against collaborationist leaders after 1890 before the entry of anarchists into the unions. The CGT was founded in 1895 by Guesdists, Blanquists and Allemanists. Most secretaries of the *Bourses du travail*, local trades councils, were socialists—three-quarters in 1911. CGT regions of strength were also socialist ones. The CGT adopted the formula of party neutrality and often elected anarchist leaders precisely because its members were divided over political strategy.[47] After failed confrontations with the government from the general strike of 1 May 1906 to the railway strike of 1910, the CGT became less hostile to the socialists, cooperating with them in a campaign to avert the war.

Historians have given too much credence to government claims that reformists outnumbered revolutionaries in the CGT.[48] Reformism as such was never an option. The *Revue syndicaliste* of the moderate faction edited by Albert Thomas manifested only tactical differences with the CGT leadership. Those who doubted the success of the general strike controlled the largest federations, mining and rail, but they were being challenged by revolutionary factions before 1914. France was still a desert for collective bargaining because of the weakness of reformism in the unions and the fears of the bourgeoisie.[49] There was a crisis of both syndicalism and parliamentary socialism before 1914 as both appeared to reach their limits of recruitment. Most leaders believed the solution lay in better organisation and more co-operation with the republic, but a minority at least—anarchosyndicalists in the CGT and Allemanists in the Socialist Party—thought that collaboration with—and infiltration by—the government was part of the problem. Reformist tendencies but not reformism were in the ascendancy before the war. While the revolutionary general strike had obviously failed as a tactic, generalised mass strikes and radical industrial unions had proven themselves more effective than smaller sectional strikes and craft unions in achieving immediate results.[50]

The First World War, by mobilising the military and civilian population and extending the reach of the state into social and economic life, created the conditions both for the regime integration of the more reformist elements who stayed with the Socialist Party and CGT and the revolt of revolutionary ones who formed the Communist Party. Until war weariness set in in 1917, only an extreme minority questioned the justice of the French cause. During the first three years of the war socialists joined the government and unions collaborated with the state and employers on arbitration commissions. The government and socialist minister of armaments, Thomas, responded to the strikes that broke out in 1917 by fixing minimum wages, negotiating collective agreements, extending arbitration and introducing worker delegates in the armaments factories. The Clemenceau government of 1917 combined more severe repression against anti-war activists with sympathy for union delegates and strikers for whom the state was both in varying degrees a friend and an enemy.[51]

The war separated out the friends and enemies of the republican state in the labour movement. There were already signs of tension in 1914 between political and union leaders who were becoming more accommodating to the government and rank and file militants. Most leaders supported the war effort. But the anti-war minority found a growing restless audience in the large armaments and other factories, especially those that proliferated in the suburbs outside the control of union and party bureaucracies. The minority of the metal workers' union called a strike during the German offensive of Spring 1918. It was those workers who put their class interest above that of the state in this situation, those who struck during the last two years of the war and those who attended the 1918 congress of the CGT in the face of government repression who formed the Communist Party.[52]

The party was founded in December 1920 at Tours in the wake of the enthusiasm generated by the advance of the Red Army into Poland after the defeat of the left in the elections of 1919 and the failure of a general railway strike in May 1920.[53] The war and Russian Revolution had not produced a revolutionary situation in France, but had caused a profound split in the labour movement. A majority of socialists, especially the young and working class, voted to join the Third International; partisans of joining did particularly well relative to their union strength where socialist organisation was weak. The reasons most frequently cited by delegates at Tours for adhesion was their hostility to parliamentarians who had grown distant from the rank and file with wartime collaboration that had only strengthened the ruling class.[54]

The communist-led CGTU was formed by those workers militant enough to defy the state in wartime. They came from both the poorly organised unstable trades like construction, dress-making, and hairdressing, which were influenced by anarcho-syndicalism and which rebelled against communist control, and more permanently from large-scale industries that had expanded during the war—metallurgical, chemical, mining and railways. The communists captured the revolutionary aspirations that wartime experience had generated among industrial workers. Workers from the more protected public and semi-public sectors—teachers, civil servants, postmen, gas and electricity employees on the one hand and miners and railwaymen on the other—tended to remain loyal to the CGT and socialists until reunification under the Popular Front.[55]

The communists asserted their independence by breaking with the tradition of republican discipline whereby socialists supported the best-placed republican on the second round of elections against the right. Nevertheless, communists struck their first electoral roots in the old republican bastions of the Parisian region, north and west Massif Central, and Midi plus the industrial North, which had been conquered by the Guesdists. Their attacks on socialists as accomplices of fascism during the 'third period' further depleted their ranks and confirmed their role as spoilers of the republican left.

The Popular Front changed them from being spoilers to leaders of the republican left. When in order to defeat fascism Maurice Thorez, secretary-general of the party, extended a hand to the radicals in October 1934, against the wishes of the Comintern, he was reaching out to the republican peasantry and middle classes and assuming for his party the historic mantle of 1792. Through the Comintern the strategy of the Popular Front, which was originally designed for French conditions, was transmitted around the world with far-reaching consequences from Spain to China.[56]

For those who identify the party with Stalinist purges, it is difficult to see it as the party of republican democracy after 1934, but it was the foremost defender of representative democracy against fascism in France. Witness historian Agulhon, austere Protestant from the Gard and Cévennes, who joined the party at the *Ecole normale* in 1946 because it seemed to be the most authentically republican.[57] The Cold War split the Popular Front alliance, driving most republican and socialist parties into an alliance with the right and practically eliminating the Communist Party in some countries. But the very orthodox French communists, drawing on republican values and traditions, survived the Cold War as the leader of the left, retaining the allegiance of one-quarter of the electorate.[58]

Social alliances and regional bastions

The geographical continuity of the French left was first explored by André Siegfried, a founder of French political science.[59] He noted a variety of material and social factors, richness of soil, population concentration, land ownership, and independence from the church and nobility that explained why some peasants in Britanny became republicans rather than royalists. He generalised his findings to a theory of two Frances, one traditional and hierarchical, the other egalitarian and democratic.

William Brustein, an American sociologist, has statistically tested and confirmed Siegfried's intuitions for agricultural France.[60] Consolidating several of Siegfried's explanatory factors, Brustein delineates at least three predominant regional modes of production, the hierarchical West, the egalitarian Midi and northern plains, which changed from being republican in 1849 to the moderate right. The decisive factors were land tenure and wealth and openness to urban markets. The grove-enclosed *bocages* and isolated hamlets of the West that were hermetically sealed off from the towns remained under the thumb of the local clergy and nobility, whereas the small-holding vintners of the Midi were drawn into republican politics because they sold to a volatile market and lived among workers and artisans in the market towns. The northern plains were transformed with the help of the grain tariff from a variegated region of tenants, sharecroppers and labourers many of whom voted 'red' in 1849 to a prosperous region of relatively large farmers, who became Orleanist or moderate republican.

Not all French regions were as polarised politically as Britanny and the Midi, but whether moderately conservative like Normandy and the Northern plains or momentarily Bonapartist like the south-west the political allegiances of localities can be explained over the long-term by a combination of religious and material factors and virtually all regions and urban districts classified as right or left.[61] Left allegiance was determined by a combination of anti-clericalism and class, the former enforcing materialist values and highlighting the salience of the latter.

In the course of a century the socialist left—ideology and social alliance—successively assumed the mantle of the 'démoc-socs' of 1849, the radical-socialists of 1881, the socialists of 1914 and the communists of 1946. It retained a social core of urban workers and small-holding peasants and the regional heartlands of the South-east, Midi, and the northern, western and south-western slopes of the Massif Central to which was added after the phylloxera the lower Midi and after the break-up of Boulangism the industrial North. The class and regional core of the left survived through the Fifth Republic until 1978 and traces remain in the communist vote today.[62] It was broken up by the emergence after 1968 of a new Socialist Party that, while preserving a Marxist rhetoric, appealed to all classes but the bourgeoisie, especially the salaried middle-class, newly industrialised workers and property-owning Catholics of diminishing faith.[63]

The socialists were able to draw upon large-scale socio-economic and cultural changes in French society that were common to most industrial countries, namely the decline of the peasantry and rise of the salaried middle classes—public and service sector workers, technicians, and lower management—the loss of religious faith, and the disaggregation and reduction of the industrial working class, particularly the skilled workers who were the stalwarts of communism. French Catholicism, which had acquired its anti-statist and propertied orientation in two centuries of battles with socialism, was the cultural bridge between newly industrialised workers and salaried middle classes who together formed the 'second left' in the Socialist Party and CFDT union confederation.

With support from these new forces the socialists were able to distance the communists in 1978 and render them impotent after the 1981 election of François Mitterrand as president. Represented in government by Rocard, Jacques Delors and Pierre Mauroy, the planning, finance and prime ministers respectively, these forces were able to veto the prolongation of Mitterrand's nationally oriented socialist policies and to induce a turn toward Europe that yielded the single market and currency.[64] By assuming leadership of the left as an inter-classist, culturally pluralistic party whose electoral profile bore greater resemblance to Radicalism, the socialists interrupted historical continuities and undermined traditional social and regional bases held by the communists. For much of the working class weaned from the communists, a vote for the socialists was a way-station toward hostile abstention and the anti-immigrant National Front, which by the mid-1990s was attracting the largest percentage of worker votes of any French party.[65]

The long view

Drawing upon more local and detailed studies the long view of history may uncover structural supports, foundational events and continuities that lie undetected in more limited studies. The long view, which was developed by the *Annales* school in the realms of geographic, climatic and economic history, has rarely been applied to politics.[66] Furet said he gave up *Annales* history for politics because he was interested in the realm of freedom not necessity and the lessons that history held for contemporaries. Though he focused his attention on the role of great men in politics, he also highlighted, to begrudge it on the left, the constraining ideological traditions of the past.[67]

This article has explored the continuities of the French left from a more materialist viewpoint seeking to uncover both its structural supports and the defining moments.[68] The structural supports must be explained not just in relational terms of class, but in the specific material and ideological conditions that tended to bring out class action and consciousness such as geographical concentration and proximity, market relations and craft solidarities on the one hand and anti-clericalism and the pre-industrial ideology of republicanism on the other. The defining moments or events in France were the Revolution of 1789, which set off a process of permanent struggle of bourgeois factions allied with urban and rural populace against monarchy, church and privileged classes, and the revolution of 1848 in which republicans relied on workers to overthrow the July Monarchy only to be pushed aside in 1849 by more radical elements who forged a socialist alliance of petty bourgeois, workers and peasants.

This alliance with its regional bastions endured the transformations of republicanism into socialism, syndicalism and communism until at least 1978. Only the theoretical and organisational forms, reflecting the growth of the working class and disillusionment with republican regimes, shifted—from an idealist Rousseauist republicanism led by middle-class radicals to Marxist workers' parties; the values, programmes, geography and social alliances remained essentially the same. The Communist Party, built within an organisational structure exported from the Soviet revolution, came to embody the historic continuities of French republicanism until challenged in the 1970s by a Socialist Party drawing upon the growth of the salaried middle class and the secularisation of Catholics. But the decline of communism left a legacy of popular anti-capitalist feeling and militancy that still sets France off from other Western nations and a pluralist left under Jospin that is governing under the traditional sign of the republic.[69]

This article is based on a talk given at the ASMCF Annual Conference, Cardiff University, 2–4 September 1999.

Notes

Unless otherwise specified all books in French are published in Paris.

1. *Le Monde*, 21 June 1997.
2. F. Venturi, *Historiens du XXe siècle* (Geneva, 1966), pp.5–55.
3. J. Jaurès (ed.), *Histoire socialiste*, 12 vols., 1900–1908, esp. XII, pp.306–12; V. Lecoulant, 'Naissance d'une oeuvre: *L'Histoire socialiste de la Révolution française*', *Bulletin de la Société d'études jaurèsiennes*, no. 119 (Oct.-Dec. 1990), pp.4–13.
4. See the bibliographical essay in my *The Origins of the French Labor Movement: the socialism of skilled workers, 1830–1914* (Berkeley, CA, 1976), pp.201–10.
5. M. Agulhon, *The Republican Experiment, 1848–52* (Cambridge, 1983), *La République, 1880–1932* (1990); J.-P. Bertaud et al. (eds), *Histoire de la France contemporaine*, 8 vols (1978–81); F. Furet, *La Révolution de Turgot à Jules Ferry, 1770–1880* (1988), transl. as *Revolutionary France, 1770–1880* (Oxford, 1992).
6. Edmund Burke, *Reflections on the Revolution in France*, especially the introduction by Conor Cruise O'Brien (London, 1968 edn).
7. Cf. J. Talmon, *The Origins of Totalitarian Democracy* (London, 1952), and Furet, *Revolutionary France*.
8. Modernists like M. Gauchet, 'Right and Left', in P. Nora (ed.), *Realms of Memory: rethinking the French past* (New York, 1996), deny this coherence and continuity.
9. J.-P. Gross, *Fair Shares for all: Jacobin egalitarianism in practice* (Cambridge, 1997). M. Vovelle, *Les Jacobins de Robespierre à Chevènement* (1999), ch.1. J. Boutier and P. Boutry, *Atlas de la Révolution française, Sociétés populaires*, vol.6 (1992).
10. Moss, *French Labor Movement*, ch.3.
11. Cited by B. Moss, 'Marx and the permanent revolution in France: background to the *Communist Manifesto*', in C. Leys and L. Panitch (eds), *Socialist Register 1998* (Woodbridge, 1998), p.157.
12. *Ibid.*, pp.147–68; also B. Moss, 'Marx and Engels on French social democracy: historians or revolutionaries?', *Journal of the History of Ideas*, vol.46 (1985), pp.539–57.
13. According to C. Church, *Revolution and Red Tape: the French ministerial bureaucracy* (Oxford, 1981), the Jacobins created centralized ministries, but Napoléon made them 'bureaucratic'.
14. See L. Ferry and A. Renaut, *68–86, itinéraires de l'individu* (1987), and H. Weber, *Vingt ans après, que reste-t-il de 68?* (1988).
15. Moss, 'Marx and Permanent Revolution'. Marx's model is largely substantiated by Albert Soboul, *The French Revolution, 1789–1799: from the storming of the Bastille to Napoleon* (London, 1989).

16. Moss, 'Marx and permanent Revolution'.

17. Cf. G. Lefranc, *Les Gauches en France, 1789–1972* (1973), p.17; A. Soboul (ed.), *Girondins et montagnards: actes de colloque, 14 décembre 1975* (1980).

18. Cf. E.M. Woods, 'The state and popular sovereignty in French political thought: a genealogy of Rousseau's "General Will"', in F. Krantz (ed.), *History from Below: studies in popular protest and popular ideology* (Montreal, 1985), pp.130–42; A. Soboul, *Les Sans-culottes parisiens en l'an II. Mouvement populaire et gouvernement révolutionnaire, 2 juin 1793–9 thermidor an II* (1958); Soboul, 'Classes populaires et rousseauisme sous la Révolution', *Annales historiques de la Révolution française* 34 (1962), pp.421–38.

19. *Histoire de la conspiration pour l'égalité, dite de Babeuf* (Brussels, 1828). Albert Mathiez was the only major historian who noticed Robespierre's redistributive policy, J. Friguglietti, *Albert Mathiez: historien révolutionnaire* (Paris, 1974), pp.197–210.

20. J.-M. Schiappa, *Gracchus Babeuf avec les Egaux* (1991). I. Birchall, *The Spectre of Babeuf* (London, 1997).

21. S. Bernstein, *Blanqui and the Art of Insurrection* (London, 1971), pp.59–62.

22. *Histoire du parti républicain en France de 1814–1870* (1900). J. Gilmore, *La République clandestine, 1818–1848* (1992), esp. pp.159–228, is the work of an American amateur.

23. Boutier and Boutry, *Atlas*. I. Woloch, *Jacobin Legacy: the democratic movement under the Directory* (Princeton, NJ, 1970).

24. S. Vila, 'Luttes populaires dans l'Hérault, 1830–34', in *Droite et gauche de 1789 à nos jours* (Montpellier, 1975). Gilmore, *République clandestine*, pp.159–228.

25. B. Moss. 'Parisian workers and the origins of republican socialism, 1830–33', in J. Merriman (ed.), *1830 in France* (New York, 1975).

26. J.-P. Aguet, *Les Grèves sous la Monarchie de Juillet (1830–1847)* (Geneva, 1954). The proletarianised woollen workers of Lodève, culturally still Catholic, appear to have acted independently of republicans, C. Johnson, *The Life and Death of Industrial Languedoc, 1700–1920* (London, 1995).

27. P. Stearns, *Paths to Authority: the middle class and the industrial labor force in France, 1820–1848* (Urbana, IL, 1978).

28. E.g. D. Lindenberg, *Le Marxisme introuvable* (1975); Moss, 'Marx and permanent revolution'.

29. We still do not have an adequate history of the Second Republic but see Agulhon, *Republican Experiment* and F. Demier and J.-L. Mayaud (eds), 'Cinquantes Ans de Recherches sur 1848', *Revue d'histoire du XIXe siècle*, no. 14 (1997).

30. R. Gosselin, *Les Almanachs républicains: traditions révolutionnaires et culture politique des masses populaires de Paris, 1840–1851* (1992).

31. B. Moss, 'Radicalism and social reform in France: progressive employers and the Comité Mascuraud', *French History,* vol.11 (1997), pp.170–89. For variations of bourgeois relations with workers see R. Aminzade, *Ballots and Barricades: class formation and republican politics in France, 1830–71* (Princeton, NJ, 1993).

32. P. McPhee, *A Social History of France, 1780–1880* (London, 1992), pp.152–3.

33. P. Vigier, *La Seconde République dans la Région alpine* (1963), II, pp.62–3, 148–52, 201, and his *La Vie quotidienne en province et Paris pendant les journées de 1848, 1847–1851* (1982). P. Barral, *Les Agrariens français de Méline à Pisani* (1968), pp.41–63. M. Vigreux, 'Comportements révolutionnaires en Morvan central au milieu du XIXe siècle: structures foncières, sociales et mentales, souvenir de l'Ancien Régime et de la Révolution', *Annales historiques de la Révolution française*, no.274 (1988), pp.427–43. *Droite et gauche de 1789 à nos jours*. P. Lévêque, *Une Société en crise: la Bourgogne au milieu du XIXe siècle (1846–1852)* (1983).

34. Cf. P. McPhee, *The Politics of Rural Life: political mobilization in the French countryside, 1848–52* (London, 1992), which is less structurally oriented.

35. B. Moss, 'La Première Internationale, la coopération et le mouvement ouvrier à Paris (1865–1871): le mythe du Proudhonisme', *Cahiers d'histoire de l'I.R.M.*, no.37 (1989), pp.33–48.

36. M. Johnson, T*he Paradise of Association: political culture and popular organization in the Paris Commune of 1871* (Ann Arbor, 1996).

37. J. Rougerie, *Procès des communards* (1964), 'L'A.I.T. et le mouvement ouvrier à Paris pendant les évènements de 1870–71', *International Review of Social History* 17 (1972), pp.3–102, and his essay in *La Commune de 1871: actes 1971* (1972), pp.62–79. Also M. Allner, 'Les Communaux jacobins: héritage idéologique et exercise du pouvoir révolutionnaire', *Le Mouvement social*, no. 117 (1981), pp.76–103.

38. J. Labusquière, *La Troisième République*, vol. XII, *Histoire socialiste*, pp.166–9.

39. J. Néré, 'La Crise industrielle de 1882 et le mouvement boulangiste', 2 vols. (Thèse d'état, Université de Paris, 1959). N. Fitch, 'Mass culture, mass parliamentary politics and modern anti-semitism: The Dreyfus affair in rural France', *American Historical Review*. vol.97 (1991), pp.55-95. P. Nord, *Paris Shopkeepers and the Politics of Resentment* (Princeton, N.J., 1986); O. Rudelle, *La République absolue, 1870–1889: aux origines de l'instabilité constitutionnelle de la Troisième République* (1982).

40. *Workers on Strike, France 1871–1890* (Oxford, 1987).

41. Moss, *French Labor Movement*, chs 3–5; also Moss, 'Political origins of revolutionary syndicalism', *Proceedings of the Western Society for the Study of French History* 2 (1976), pp.200–10.

42. *Edouard Vaillant: la création de l'unité socialiste en France* (1982).

43. Venturi, *Historiens*, pp.30–33. Jaurès, *Discours parlementaire* (1904), pp.174–6, claims he was a collectivist even then.

44. Moss, 'Radicalism and social reform in France'.

45. G. Friedman, 'Strike success and union ideology: the US and France, 1880–1914', *Journal of Economic History*, vol.48 (1988), pp.1–15, and his *State-making and Labor Movements: France and the United States, 1876–1914* (Ithaca, NY, 1998).

46. The leading historian of syndicalism, Jacques Julliard, *Fernand Pelloutier et les origines du syndicalisme d'action directe* (1971), was a major promoter of the 'second left'.

47. Moss, *French Labor Movement*, ch.5; Moss, 'Origins of revolutionary syndicalism'.

48. Cf. L. Lorwin, *Syndicalism in France* (New York, 1914).

49. Cf. P. Stearns, *Revolutionary Syndicalism and French Labor: a cause without rebels* (New

Brunswick, NJ, 1971), and his 'Against the strike threat: employer policy toward labor agitation in France, 1900–1914', *Journal of Modern History,* vol.40 (1968), pp.474–500 with J. M. Arniou, *Evolution des conventions collectives du travail* (1938); Friedman, 'Strike success'; Friedman, *State-Making and Labor.*

50. Friedman, *State-Making and Labor.* S. Cohen, *When Strikes Make Sense—and Why: lessons from the Third Republic coal miners* (New York, 1993).

51. J.-L. Robert, *Les Ouvriers, la patrie et la révolution à Paris, 1914–1919* (1995).

52. *Ibid*; and Robert, *La Scission syndicale de 1921* (1980).

53. Annie Kriegel, *Aux Origines du Communisme francais*, 2 vols (1964), only looked at the conjunctural reasons for Communist success.

54. Jean Charles et al. (eds), *Le Congrès de Tours (texte intégral)* (1980).

55. Robert, *Scission* . M. Dreyfus, *Histoire de la CGT: cent Ans du syndicalisme en France* (1995), pp.139–40.

56. S. Wolikow, *Le Front populaire en France* (1996). R. Bourderon et al., *Le PCF: étapes et problèmes* (1981).

57. In S. Nora (ed.), *Essais d'ego-histoire* (1987), pp.23–59.

58. See opinion poll in *Temps modernes*, nos. 112–13 (1955), pp.1576–1625.

59. *Tableau politique de la France de l'Ouest sous la Troisième République* (1913).

60. *The Social Origins of Political Regionalism, France, 1849–1981* (Berkeley, CA, 1988).

61. Religion was a better predictor of voting than class even under the Fifth Republic, G. Michalat, and M. Simon, *Classe, religion et comportement politique* (1977), but the work of Siegfried and Brustein suggest that even religious faith may be explained by material factors in the past.

62. E. Labrousse, 'Géographie du socialisme', *Revue socialiste*, no.1 (1946), pp.137–48. F. Goguel, *Géographie des élections francaises sous la Troisième et la Quatrième République* (1970).

63. J. Jaffré, 'Les Structures du vote socialiste en 1973', (DES, Université de Paris I, 1973). J. Capdevielle et al., *France de gauche, vote à droite* (1981). A. Lancelot (ed.), *1981: les elections de l'alternative* (1986).

64. B. Moss and J. Michie (eds), *The Single European Currency in National Perspective: A Community in Crisis?* (London, 1998), ch.3.

65. P. Perrineau., 'Dynamique du vote Le Pen: le poids du "gaucho-lepenisme"' in P. Perrineau and C. Ysmal (eds), *Vote de crise* (1995).

66. F. Dosse, *New History in France: The Triumph of the Annales* (Urbana, IL, 1994).

67. F. Furet, *L'Atelier de l'histoire* (1982); Furet, *La Révolution.*

68. Cf. M. Vovelle, 'Ruptures et continuité dans l'histoire de la France contemporaine', in *Histoire de la France contemporaine*, vol.8.

69. D. Boy and N. Mayer (eds), *L'Electeur a ses raisons* (1997), pp.14, 62.

The Artist as Subversive?
The Russian *avant-garde* and the state, 1905–1924

Judith Harrison and Liam O'Sullivan

> That purely individualistic irony which spreads out like a smoke of indifference over the whole effort and intention of mankind is the worst form of snobbism. It rings false alike in artistic creations and works of history. But there is an irony deep laid in the very relations of life. It is the duty of the historian as of the artist to bring it to the surface.
>
> *Leon Trotsky*

It was a central idea of Bolshevism, and of Lenin in particular, that it was the very lateness of the development of capitalism in Russia and its accelerating speed by the beginning of the twentieth century that made the country the possible site of revolutionary breakthrough into a new social order. In apparent paradox, the very backwardness of what was to be made into the Soviet Union gave the latecomer the possibility of pride of place in the extreme circumstances of 1917. Within the space of a single lifetime Russia had moved from medieval feudalism through nineteenth century capitalism to socialist revolution as though epochs could be collapsed into years, years into weeks or even days.

Politics came to be seen, at least within those small circles, as a matter of total urgency. Action guided by will and rapidly constructed theory was of the essence so that the time could be seized, revolutionary power organised and the reaction averted. Given the extraordinary circumstances and a rapidly changing 'parallelogram of forces', a coincidence of utmost necessity and danger and utmost enthusiasm might push forward to the emergence of a new kind of civilisation and a new epoch based on working-class power throughout the capitalist world, a world already close to barbarism in the cataclysm of military dictatorships clashing in the vast imperialist war. Outcomes in Russia could be decisive for the struggle in the capitalist world as a whole and also exemplary. That such an analysis should prevail through force of ideas and force of arms and have a shaping impact upon the history of the twentieth century remains astonishing. Very few, even within the leadership of the Bolshevik party, could have thought through the implications of this analysis or foreseen its consequences and the ruthless struggles around its conscious application.

Many radicals embraced the idea that a revolution of workers and peasants would give rise to a new world whose time had somehow come. Many intimations of a moral, intellectual and indeed aesthetic and spiritual revolution, a practical realisation, in a way, of Enlightenment abstractions, in the very rapid transition from absolutism to modernity were widely discerned. Particularly was this so among aspiring intellectuals and artists. In the circumstances of 1917 it was very widely doubted that the meliorative or liberal solutions which had been long in the making through a multitude of social crises in more advanced societies could be in any way adequate to the social catastrophe and revolutionary pressures experienced in Russia. Few anticipated the enormous sea change that was to transform their whole world, but many were enthusiastic for it. And the extraordinary artistic and intellectual ferment which preceded 1917, in which many flowers bloomed—and often faded—could in itself be seen as an accelerated and more intense version of what was happening elsewhere in more advanced societies. The ground to be made was altogether greater, the speed of change was more intense, the concentration of talents, of social experiment, thought experiment, of political extreme, proselytising energy, social and cultural variety, foreign influence, depth and rapidity of achievement, political oppression and social frustration were all stronger. As was also the depth of religious tradition, as well as the ferocity of prejudice, superstition and pogroms. The gulf between metropolitan innovation and decadence, and rural tradition, was a point of polarisation for artistic and moral enthusiasm.

Russian exceptionalism and particularity was manifest to all observers— half a million semi-autonomous villages scattered across one-sixth of the world's habitable surface, together with the dynamism and growing sophistication of the cities, with overwhelming concentration of energy in Moscow and Petersburg.[1] And the axis of modernity versus tradition, the contrast between progressive, innovative and enlightened Westernising tendencies and the authenticity, vivacity and warmth of peasant life had become highly developed in what was often seen as a struggle for the Russian soul and for justice and happiness.

The interplay between the artistic *avant-garde* and the political *avant-garde* in Russia is replete with extraordinary ironies, with damaged lives, tragic fates, bitter defeats, extraordinary drama, limitless adversity, amazing survivals and escapes, and also with vivid and still luminous achievements. There were many decisive interventions in the field of creative expression whose impact continues; deep clashes of viewpoint and conception which reverberate to the present day—a profusion of influences whose course has not yet run. It was also, let it never be forgotten, an era of enormous fun, energy, zaniness and optimism. In the pre-revolutionary situation there seemed everything to play for against an unknowable future.

In a wide variety of artistic fields and across a very broad spectrum of genre and media, with burgeoning profusion, a flood of new developments were brought to fruition by a new generation of creative workers. They appeared not only in painting, in sculpture and the plastic arts, in design and architecture, poetry, drama, theatre and stage design, dance, music and other performance arts, photography and film, but also in art education and administration and in the creation of new media and modes of expression and communication. In some ways, this great birth and seed time had to do with Russian artists embracing and quickly learning from developments across Europe associated with the emergence of 'modernism'—with a rapid assimilation of new currents and influences and the capacity to take many of those currents and influences in distinctive directions. In other ways it involved more clearly native developments which quickly fed into the new streams of world culture in a diaspora of fresh ideas and influences. And all of this took place within a rapidly changing and crisis-ridden political atmosphere laden with both optimism and menace; the eternal ambiguity between political power and artistic expression came to present itself with ever-increasing sharpness.

The spiritual and intellectual cross-currents to which aspiring artists and intellectuals in Russia came to be increasingly exposed were laden with unresolved tension and complexity. Many paradigmatic shifts were occurring throughout industrial societies with the dawn of the new century. They were visible in the sciences, notably in physics, but also in chemistry and biology; in philosophy and logic and in a different register within metaphysics; in psychology, with new and antagonistic schools coming to the fore; and in the rise of literally spectacular technical advances such as motor transport, flight, and all manner of changes associated with the use of electricity for light and power; in medicine and medical technology, all within an increasingly scientistic and materialistic frame of reference accompanied by new means of production and new material and technical possibilities. And with the deepening of scientism, and various kinds of hubris associated with it, emerged far-reaching and often esoteric efforts to create or discover spiritual or 'religious' complements, correlates or alternatives to it. This was true even within Marxism itself.

Reading the cross-currents

One aspect of the artistic transformations that were wrought in the early decades of the twentieth century which have so profoundly transformed our sensorium has been the entirely controversy-ridden character of those developments. Critical, commercial, and perhaps most spectacularly, political mediation of shifts in the realm of artistic expression have been highly verbal, spawning vocabularies, labels and code words which serve as rallying points or gestures for a host of competing purposes. Sometimes they have been grounded in fairly well worked-out manifestos, sometimes on the basis of slogans adopted for polemical purposes. As a way into examining some of the multiple cross-currents which marked the rich and varied careers of ideas and tendencies in the life of what is typically called the *avant-garde* in Russia it is necessary to draw upon those various terms and terminologies. But this must always be with the warning that the changing polemics may conceal as much as they reveal.

A flood of new modern painting from Western Europe was very soon transported to Russia through the purchases of wealthy businessmen forming the basis of still-important collections. By the early years of the century, in a reciprocal movement, the *Ballets Russes* of Diaghilev impacted upon the West and continued to be an important focus for many of the arts in a distinctively Russian cosmopolitanism. The movement of ideas and objects, but more importantly of people, carried crucial messages of new possibilities across the divide between Russia and the West. Two more or less simultaneous developments in painting and the plastic arts—Cubism, pioneered by Picasso and Braque, and Italian Futurism—were quickly taken up, assimilated and built upon. Inasmuch as Cubism had a definite conceptual, as opposed to a perceptual, basis, this was largely worked out theoretically by critics and writers rather than by its founders, who were more concerned to show rather than to say. Its revolutionary impact, somehow in the shadow of Cezanne, was quite immediate, depending as much as anything upon the energies of patrons and dealers. Futurism was highly verbal, eventful and propagandist and dependent upon the promotion and self-promotion of its protagonists, notably Marinetti. Picasso and his vivid circle spoke as anarchists at that time, with a certain amount of Nietzschean sloganeering. The Futurists were fairly unmistakably proto-Fascist.

The first abstract painters

Two painters, Mikhail Larionov and Natalya Goncharova, who had already exhibited in Paris under the aegis of Diaghilev and were seen as celebrators of themes and influences from Russian folk art, were sharply influenced. So, indeed, were a whole group of younger contemporaries, very frequently women, whose achievements and careers will shortly be discussed. Although their contributions were far too distinctive and original to allow them to be thought of as merely derivative, they quickly described themselves as 'Cubofuturists'. In 1913 Larionov had issued his Rayonist manifesto. Rayonism as an idea was based upon claims regarding the physical energies of colour and the intersection of colour planes. And in fact Larionov and Goncharova, who worked on the productions of Diaghilev in Paris, can be accounted the first abstract painters. Although the manifesto stressed painterly values over and above representation and imagery, its tone was strongly Futurist:

> We exclaim: the whole brilliant style of modern times—our trousers, jackets, shoes, trolleys, cars, airplanes, railways, grandiose steamships....Long live nationality! We march hand in hand with our ordinary house-painters...Here begins the true freeing of painting and its life in accordance with its own laws, a self-sufficient painting, with its own forms, colour and timbre.[2]

Futurism was in its way scientistic, based upon the depiction of speed and movement, as discernible in fact through the discoveries of photography. Some of Goncharova's work was fairly clearly influenced by the Futurist Balla. But great contrasts may be made with other ways in which that particular kind of interest was taken in entirely different directions—in very strong repudiation of the ideological preoccupations of the Italians. Larionov suggested to a journalist, before his visit to Russia in 1914, that an appropriate welcome for Marinetti might be to pelt him with rotten eggs.

Most sharply is this contrast clear in the life work of Naum Gabo, who acknowledged the discoveries of the Italians. A founder of the Constructivist movement, Gabo, together with his brother Antoine Pevsner, was later to declare in 'The realist manifesto' which they posted on walls in 1920:

> Look at a ray of sun...the stillest of the still forces, it speeds more than 300 kilometres in a second...behold our starry firmament...who hears it and yet what are our depots to those depots of the Universe? What are our earthly trains to those hurrying trains of the galaxies?

Indeed, the Futurist noise about speed is too obvious an anecdote, and from the moment that Futurism proclaimed that 'Space and Time are yesterday's dead', it sunk into the obscurity of abstractions.

Neither Futurism nor Cubism has brought us what our time has expected of them.[3]

A deeper sense of the 'new physics' brought about a new sense of line, of space, of time, of colour, of motion, and of the appropriateness of engineering techniques and modern industrial materials from which art should be constructed. Gabo too left the Soviet Union in 1922 but he adhered to his artistic convictions throughout a long life spent at first in Germany, then in Britain and finally in the United States. The events of his life never touched his utopian optimism, it should be noted. Nor did he ever lose the warm feelings which he had experienced in the brief time in which he had been involved with workers' training and education in the civil war period.

The sense of the spiritual implication of new possibilities was by no means limited to the strict dimensions of public science. Intertwined with the developments so far briefly canvassed was a widespread apprehension that the new era might see a far-reaching awakening of the human spirit. The growth of interest in various forms of mysticism and the occult; the emergence of Theosophy and the teachings of Madame Blavatsky; wide-ranging attempts to reconcile science with religion, as for example in the teachings of Rudolf Steiner and his Anthroposophy, had a diffuse as well as a very direct impact on developments in the arts both within Russia and elsewhere. New theories of colour in terms of their psychological and emotional meanings developed by Vassily Kandinsky, whose work *Concerning the Spiritual in Art* was first published in 1912, had a profound impact on twentieth century painting and design.[4] Theosophical ideas and notions of a 'higher' physical reality, and transcendent conceptions of time and space promulgated by Ouspensky in widely attended lectures in Petersburg, shaped the work of Kasimir Malevich and the development of Suprematism. A jostle of competing scientific and parascientific ideas forced themselves in rapid succession into important streams of the art of the Russian *avant-garde* as an art which would be the end of art. And all of this occurred within a revolutionary atmosphere which sought both to raise the standards of civilisation of peasants and workers and to institute the arts of the future; a proletarian art as never before seen which would bring art into life and thus undermine its separate existence. Within the many fault lines of the *avant-garde* the possibility of rivalry, struggles for ascendency and also new possibilities for cooperation and ideological partisanship—with all the new work to be done—proliferated.

Art as politics

By the turn of the twentieth century the visual arts in Russia had already established quite a strong anti-authoritarian tradition. A new realistic commitment, stimulated in part by Chernyshevsky, had given a definite social purpose to the Wanderers, most notably and famously Ilya Repin, who had turned their backs on academy art cast in a classical heroic mould for its Western character, taking art to the people and away from the galleries of Moscow and Petersburg.[5] Depicting themes from ordinary life, sometimes within a very highly achieved realism, this work in asserting itself as radical took up a position on the political spectrum—even though it took little notice of peasant artistic work in itself. A fully elaborated assimilation of *fin de siècle* Western themes in art, literature, poetry and design, a strong and distinctive growth of symbolism, in reaction to realistic currents, pressed Russian arts and artists into deeper contact with modernity and late Bohemianism. Art had become, in the Russian context, increasingly and consciously a political activity.

After the disappointments of 1905, artists vied for supremacy over the nature and future of art as political theorists and activists were arguing over the direction of the revolution. Both groups were in conflict with the autocracy and art exhibitions reflected the underlying controversies. A decisive intervention in this respect arose from the outstanding collections of modern painting assembled in Moscow. The wealthy Sergei Shchukin purchased and displayed from the beginning of the century until the outbreak of the Great War more than two hundred modern, mostly French, paintings including a large volume of much of the latest work of Matisse from whom he had commissioned important paintings and fifty works by Picasso, as well as paintings by Monet, Renoir, Gauguin, Cezanne and Derain. His friends and rivals the Morosov family, wealthy textile mill owners, had amassed a very large number of contemporary French works to which artists had privileged access. Kandinsky helped to promote very large exhibitions of Fauvist, Expressionist and Cubist paintings organised by Vladimir Izdebsky in 1909–10. Younger Russian painters were becoming entirely familiar with the latest currents of the European *avant-garde* and vigorously beginning to promote their own. In December 1910 and January 1911 the group led by Larionov and brothers David and Vladimir Burlyuk organised the Jack of Diamonds exhibition in Moscow, mostly by younger Russians—radical work which, in John Bowlt's phrase 'moved from decorativeness and polychromy toward a more acute analysis of form and content and a more architectonic composition'.[6] Their exhibition of that year reflected both current Western developments and such consciously Russian influences as religious icons and 'primitive' peasant art and prints. By 1911 the group had split acrimoniously with Goncharova and Larionov taking up leadership of the Donkey's Tail group. They sought a deeper exploration of native Russian themes and for a more grounded respect for the preoccupations of working artists in repudiation of what they saw as an intellectualising and over-theoretical reception of Western influences. This Slavophile moment had important implications politically and even spiritually, but it was above all an artistic turn carrying artistic emphases. Indeed, Goncharova went so far as to declare

> Cubism is a positive phenomenon, but it is not altogether a new one. The Scythian stone images, the painted wooden dolls sold at fairs are those same cubist works, but in France too, the home of cubism, it was the monuments of Gothic sculpture that served as the point of departure for this movement. For a long time I have been working in the manner of cubism, but I condemn without hesitation the position of the Knave of Diamonds, which has replaced creativity with theorising.[7]

Art, apparently parodying religion, in exhibitions with such irreverent names, infuriated the authorities. Goncharova was put on trial for obscenity; one exhibition of her work was closed after a single evening, and more than once her work was censored for blasphemy.

The *avant-garde* in the pre-revolutionary period was schismatic, proselytising, and rapidly changing. Hence the second Jack of Diamonds exhibition organised by David Burlyuk in 1912, took place without Larionov, Goncharova or Malevich—whose reputation was rapidly rising. At exhibitions organised by the Union of Youth the two groups consented to show together and important new figures emerged, notably Olga Rozanova and Vladimir Tatlin. Mayakovsky, the great poet, and future dramatist and graphic artist, established himself as a painter in the 'Futurist' manner in this context. Larionov was particularly interested in the 'primitivist' style of Marc Chagall's painting and encouraged it. Chagall's expressionistic work at that time explored the Jewish world of his native Vitebsk. Larionov's group exhibition The Target in 1913 moved further in the direction of primitivism.

An important aspect of the *avant-garde* in painting was its intimacy, even fusion, with other modes of expression, with literature and theatre. Exhibitions became events, accompanied by new kinds of writing, as well as typography, illustrated books issuing forth alongside rapidly changing styles and modes of painting, with theatrical productions becoming the site of experiments in stage design, sets and costumes. Many individuals achieved high levels of proficiency in a swiftly expanding plethora of media. And if autocratic or petty-bourgeois respondents were scandalised, much fun was to be had at their expense. Developments of style and tendency pressed forward in tumbling profusion. Confident of their independent significance and distinctiveness the 'Russian Futurists', as they may be generically called, had growing confidence regarding their importance as a vanguard of overall social and cultural development and transformation. They came to believe that they would assume their place in the sun or perhaps even beyond the sun. But also they might typically see themselves as servants of change, as workers within new forms in a capacity which was both modest and dedicated.

These not always contradictory cross-currents are to be drawn out in the contrasting careers of Kazimir Malevich and Vladimir Tatlin. They are quite often seen as rival poles of influence within the rapidly rising trajectory of the *avant-garde*. Their clashing personalities, convictions, temperaments and indeed extraordinary gifts and talents reached extreme limits, not least brawls and fist fights. Tatlin declared at one time that he was unable to live in the same city as Malevich, even though never ceasing to be preoccupied with his work.

Malevich had a quite meteoric career within the *avant-garde*. He would have approved of the metaphor. As a personality extraordinarily verbal and persuasive, he was able to convince other artists of the highest calibre of the revolutionary character of his ideas and vision. He made substantial contributions to neo-primitivism, works which remain justly famous, and to Cubofuturism where he became a leading influence in the *avant-garde* after the departure of Larionov and Goncharova, even though his first conspicuous participation in an exhibition of modern art had been at the Jack of Diamonds show in Moscow only a few years before in 1910. He quickly pressed Cubofuturism to an entirely new form of expression, Suprematism, which he took to be a final stage of art that moved beyond appearances and substantial forms.

Reams of scholarship have been devoted to the analysis of Suprematism, its hermetic character, its metaphysical underpinnings, its mystical resonances, its origins. The abstract character of Suprematism, its deployment of elemental forms, the circle, the square, the cross, its geometric simplicity, leading fairly quickly to highly developed complexity and the reintroduction of colour, its stress upon purely painterly values which seemed to take it beyond painting were analysed and commented upon not least by Malevich himself. He subsequently located the emergence of the Suprematist idea as a product of the collaboration on a theatrical production of Mikhail Matyushin and Alexei Kruchenikh's Futurist opera, *Victory over the Sun*, in the Luna Park Theatre in Petersburg in December 1913. He learned much in that experience from the interplay of lighting and image as an extension of the possibilities of painting. The backdrop he designed was strongly suggestive of the geometric compositions to follow. It was an opera with a curious mixture of science fiction, allegory, and 'trans-sense'.

It was two more years before Malevich openly proclaimed Suprematism. *Black Circle* was one of the earliest canvases, painted in the same year as he was working on the stage sets for *Victory over the Sun*, but not exhibited until 1915. It is surely a coincidence of no small significance that an eclipse of the sun, visible across European Russia as annular, and close to its greatest totality in Petersburg, should have occurred in April 1912. There is other evidence that the eclipse directly inspired his work, and not just Suprematism. A Cubofuturist example of 'trans-sense', *An Englishman in Moscow*, which Malevich painted in 1914, has the words 'partial eclipse' written prominently across the canvas. Surely he placed his work beyond the sun! Malevich was both an assiduous publicist in discussing the sources and development of his ideas and at the same time rather covert and furtive about the origins of the whole matter. Nevertheless a highly developed sense of perception characterises all artistic endeavour, as the poet Victor Khlebnikov acknowledged. In 1912 this pioneer of Russian futurist writing (based on his interest in early Slavonic philology) together with Kruchenikh, developed a theory of *zaumny yazyk*, or directly expressed language, beyond the mind and the visible world, accessible to those with an artistic perception. It is *zaum* in its pictorial interpretation that has been described as 'trans-sense': art of the transrational, or 'Non-sense realism'.[8] Such an idea had its inspiration in many sources. They include the ancient tradition of speaking in tongues still practised in the Russian countryside by *dukhobory*, the theosophist theories of Blavatsky and Steiner's anthroposophy. In the same vein, the Italian Futurist's catalogue of their 1912 exhibition in Paris described the 'painting of states of mind' that would 'give the emotional ambience of a picture, the synthesis of the various abstract rhythms of every object, from which springs a fount of pictural lyricism hitherto unknown'.[9] These are some of the background themes lying behind Malevich's conviction that the artist may be gifted with higher levels of perception affording access to higher realities than the everyday. Much later, in his statement from the catalogue of the Tenth State Exhibition: Nonobjective Creation and Suprematism in 1919, Malevich wrote

The blue of the sky has been conquered by the system...I have breached the blue lampshade of colour limitations and have passed into the white beyond: follow me, comrade aviators, sail on into the depths—I have established the semaphores of Suprematism. I have conquered the lining of the coloured sky, I have plucked the calories and put them in the bag I have made, and tied it with a knot. Sail on! The white, free depths, eternity, is before you.[10]

Two Petrograd exhibitions in 1915, Tramway V and 0.10 (Zero Ten) were in their way artistic precursors of the Revolution. Subtitled the First, and the Last Futurist Exhibitions, they brought matters to a head. Tramway V, which represented all the artistic tendencies of the early revolutionary years, was riotous in its proliferation of personal manifestos, themes and arguments. The exhibitors wore red wooden spoons on their lapels in joyful mockery and as emblems. The exhibition included vivid works by the equally talented and innovative female artists Popova, Exter, and Udaltsova as well as Rozanova (who, along with Goncharova and Stepanova, have become known as Amazons of the Russian *avant-garde*).[11] Tatlin showed some of his new work, relief constructions made from a variety of materials which could be attached to a wall or strung across a corner, which attracted great attention. At 0.10 Malevich insisted on exhibiting only Suprematist works including the famous and infamous *Black Square on a White Ground*. It caused a great sensation and much offence. Tatlin was furious at these works and at their inclusion, regarding them as amateur. Malevich responded

The square is not a subconscious form. It is the creation of intuitive Reason. The face of the new art. The square is a royal child full of life. It is the first step of pure creation in art. Before it there were only naively ugly things and copies from nature.[12]

Tatlin had exhibited at the scandalous Donkey's Tail and Jack of Diamonds exhibitions and had been strongly influenced by Larionov. One of his early paintings, *Sailor* (1910) was in fact a self portrait—he had run away to sea at the age of eighteen and eked out a living in a variety of tenuous ways. He travelled to Berlin in 1913 after quarrelling with Larionov and Goncharova, supporting himself by playing the accordion. He visited Picasso and tried to attach himself as some kind of apprentice. This did not prove possible but his counter relief 'constructions' were influenced by work of Picasso that he had seen in progress. His rivalry with Malevich was acute. In 1916 he organised an exhibition in Moscow called The Store which included

Cubofuturist paintings. Work by Malevich was shown but his Suprematism excluded. Also it was at this exhibition that work by Alexander Rodchenko, later to develop photography as an art form, was shown—with obvious use of compasses and drawing instruments.

It was through the influence of Tatlin that constructivism at once came to be recognised as an independent form. It was seen by him also that it could be harnessed to the purposes of utility, upon the making or construction of objects for use. It was a vital aspect of constructivism for Tatlin, or at least an important element within it, that it came to be conjoined with the world of work, tilted towards design and the manufacture of artefacts. In this respect art and life could be fused. No longer was it the task of art to destroy the old art by surpassing it imaginatively. The end of art as a separate realm of personal expression would be carried forward by the creation of a new material culture. In at least one conception of constructivism, art came to be subsumed under the making of things, part of a collective process of manufacture organised according to communist principles, a social venture of worker-craftsmen aimed at meeting utilitarian needs. For some at least, constructivism came quite quickly to be thought of as 'productivism'; the realisation, at least in concept, of historical materialism in the age in which the worker would be begin to enter centre stage as the 'subject of history', as the inspirer of manufacture, rather than as a factor of production. Tatlin's absorbed interest in materials, their properties and interrelationships, was carried on in his response to traditional Russian icons. What interested him about them was what we might call their mixed media quality; their materials might include metal and gemstones as well as wood and pigment ('glass and iron are the new classicism equivalent to the marble of the ancients'). Tramway V and 0.10 attracted many visitors but few sales (6000 visitors for 0.10 and no sales). There was a certain will on the part of the public to be scandalised and to be shocked in decorous circles, even to enjoy being 'slapped in the face'.[13] But within this new work it was possible to discern the lineaments of real and deep changes in the visual arts and promise of real trouble to come.

With reduced numbers due to war service, and through shortages and privations the *avant-garde* continued to pursue their work across the board with growing confidence in their social relevance. Important figures such as Kandinsky returned with the onset of war but otherwise it was the beginning of a long period of increasing isolation and of separate development. New talents and a welter of innovations continued to proliferate, as did the underground of new political ideas, conflicts and alliances within the darkening gloom of the military situation. The shock of the new was by no means confined to the scandalous impact of the 'experiments' in the arts and the growing impertinence of experiments in living associated with them. Deep changes were at work at all levels of thought, politics and society in Russia. The old order was clearly in crisis. The holding operation of 1905 was clearly doomed.

Towards a new civilisation

With the coming of the revolution of 1917 the *avant-garde* characteristically embraced October as though it were in some way the realisation of their own struggles. Mayakovsky described it as 'his' revolution. For Tatlin, 'the political events of 1917 were prefigured in our art in 1914'.[14] Lunacharsky had urged artists to come to the aid of the Bolsheviks and many of them did so with great energy, often finding themselves occupying organisational roles. For a time at least the world of artistic culture in many of its multiple aspects was being run by artists. Avant-gardists pushed forward energetically in their own ways in the making of the revolution. The artists' faction, so to speak, had at first considerable leeway. Doctrinal differences, even deep ideological schisms, could be suspended. Though material pressures were dire, with famine, epidemic, shortages of crucial means and materials, and the virtual collapse of economic life, many became urgently involved. Their talents and vocations which had been confined to the critical fringes of a society whose day was past saw themselves as vitally engaged with helping the struggle to build a new one. One possibility was helping to take part in large-scale projects to celebrate and propagandise the revolution. At anniversaries, notably in 1918, vast spectacles were put on in the cities, covering streets and squares with abstract designs, flags and slogans and organising colossal pageants in an atmosphere, almost, of permanent carnival. Tatlin was in charge of organising monuments for celebrations in Moscow and at one point appealed to Lunacharsky to inform Lenin of difficulties and confusions and to clarify responsibilities as between the Moscow Soviet and the Commissariat.[15] Propaganda trains and river boats were sent from the cities decorated vividly and equipped with libraries and film projectors. Poster art burgeoned and thrived. Works of great force and vivid simplicity, produced by inspired hands such as Mayakovsky and Rodchenko, directly addressed the masses. Kiosks and booths were designed for its distribution. Agitation and propaganda, devising new vocabularies and images for communication to the masses, found a route for new forms of art addressed to a new public. A genuinely new aesthetic was in the making inspired by new technical means, documentary film, photomontage, street theatre, revolutions in stage design, and experiments in mixed media. In this sense easel painting was surpassed and, according to some, should be abandoned or even suppressed in the face of more relevant methods of mechanical reproduction. New means, new purposes, new audiences presaged the culture of a new civilisation. Great effort and experimentation was devoted by constructivists and others to 'utilitarian' purposes (the design of clothes and fabrics, furniture, ceramics, the exploration of new architectural possibilities, at first on a small scale); workers' reading rooms; display pavilions, and models and maquettes of gigantic and monumental projects—notably, Tatlin's Monument for the Third International. Some of this 'spun off' from the interaction between constructivism and theatre, notably the extraordinary and innovatory theatre of Vsevelod Meyerhold. Art was rapidly learning to speak in new languages.

It would be a mistake to believe that even the most iconoclastic innovators, judged on the basis of their polemical claims, were necessarily innocent or indeed fundamentally disrespectful of the artistic culture that they were attempting to surpass. It was clear to those who were moved by the work of the artists of the revolutionary period that their newness opened the possibility of a real transfiguration of sensibility. Only to read Mayakovsky's essay 'How to Make Verses' was to be reminded of how deeply alert he was to the necessity for constant and daily discipline of effort and of how much there was to be learned from the work and achievements of the past.[16] Only to look at a photomontage by El Lissitsky or to move within one of his Proun constructions was to be alerted to the art that is concealed by his art.[17] There was, nonetheless, a clamour from some of the *avant-garde* that the past should be abolished. But what of the cultural needs of the people? What of the question of training and education? What should be the priorities of the fledgling Soviet state now that all the shattered cultural institutions lay in its care? What choices must be made and what priorities decided? What of the future of the revolution? The *avant-garde* discussed these questions urgently, not only in magazines and bulletins but from positions of authority. Many leading figures, notably Kandinsky but others too, held quite influential positions within the emerging administrative structures.

From revolution to *realpolitik*

The early years of the Revolution were precarious in the extreme. Civil war, encirclement by enemies, economic collapse and rampant inflation, an alienated peasantry, dislocation of provisions and the constant fear of a reactionary coup were pressing preoccupations in an atmosphere of constant

emergency. Despite this, Lenin could not lose sight of wider, and specifically cultural, questions. After the Bolshevik seizure of power the arts, and
cultural matters generally, came under the auspices of two organisations,
Proletkult, the proletarian cultural-educational association, and Narkompros,
the commissariat concerned with education. Proletkult, which had been set
up in 1906 but only became effective in 1917, was relatively independent. It
was headed by Alexander Bogdanov, whose Marxist convictions Lenin considered to be wayward and idiosyncratic. Anatoly Lunacharsky, an old
Bolshevik and long-standing friend of Lenin, was in charge of Narkompros.
A man of wide general culture, particularly with respect to literature,
Lunacharsky was entirely convinced of the social significance of the arts and
the importance of cultural development. Alert to the potentialities of the
new media he enthusiastically supported the mobilisation of artists behind
agitation and propaganda—which indeed had shown itself to be an important weapon in the revolutionary cause. As early as April 1918, Lenin had
proposed that Lunacharsky—following the idea of Campanella's 1602
utopian work *City of the Sun* where the houses were covered in frescoes to
captivate the citizens—should select slogans for a similar 'monumental form
of propaganda'. With the civil war virtually won by the autumn of 1920, it
became a matter of importance to Lenin to give serious attention to the
world of art and not least to the metaphysical chaos that lay within it.

For Lenin philosophical questions were entirely fused with political theory and political theory was always seen in the light of practical urgency. Now
that the smoke of revolution was clearing it was a matter of importance to
think through the problem of cultural policy and get a grip on the state of
the arts. The whole matter was replete with confusion and the prevailing
debate needed to be clarified. Lenin held inflexible opinions concerning the
interpretation of Marxist materialism and, as always, the issues at stake were
political matters, they certainly turned on questions of power, involved personalities and relationships, were touched by questions of expediency,
allocation of extremely scarce resources and so on. It was hardly surprising
given the overtly mystical, not to say cabalistic, implications of some *avant-
garde* polemics (*zaum*, talk of spirituality, etc.) that Lenin chose to intervene
in the debate.

The debate, which has been discussed in several places, with varying
emphases, involved the issue of post-revolutionary civilisation in its
entirety—Narkompros was *The People's Commissariat of Enlightenment*, no less.[18]
The arts were only one element within that vast and crucial authority, but in
the circumstances Lenin's priority was to maintain what he saw as a rigid
purity of development, lest the possibility of the emergence of a genuinely

new, and therefore not yet knowable, post-revolutionary persona be compromised. In some ways Lunacharsky himself was exasperated by the iconoclasm of the *avant-garde*, the enthusiasm particularly among anarchist elements to make a clean sweep of bourgeois culture. Lenin's view was more forthright, apparently believing it 'nonsense that seeks to destroy what is beautiful purely on the grounds that it is old. We must preserve the beautiful, draw inspiration from it, develop the finest traditions from our culture instead of trying to invent a new culture at all costs'.[19] He was particularly critical of Proletkult, which tended to emphasise the autonomy of individual artists. In the very short preface to the second edition of *Materialism and Empirio-Criticism* he berated Bogdanov, by now head of the Proletkult, affirming that 'under the guise of proletarian culture workers are being offered bourgeois philosophical ideas while in the field of art an attempt is being made to foist ugliness and distortion upon them'.

The issue partly centred on the doctrinal argument that Lenin had already affirmed in this work. It aimed to repudiate those 'bourgeois philosophical ideas' which had been promulgated by Ernst Mach, and was published twice. Each time it was aimed at a single target: a positivist (or 'fideist') interpretation of materialism, associated with Alexander Bogdanov and Anatoly Lunacharsky and several others in the first edition, and the unfortunate Bogdanov very specifically in the second.[20] On the first occasion, 1908, it was one aspect in an ongoing thrust for leadership that Lenin had been pursuing since at least 1903 (with his first significant, if partial, victory, that of the Bolsheviks over the Mensheviks). Between 1907 and 1912 Lenin's contentions within the Bolshevik tendency itself concerned constitutional matters. When he first wrote his philosophical treatise in the summer of 1908 Lenin, in order to undermine the Marxist credentials of the opposition, personalised the constitutional debate while substituting ideology for an ongoing disagreement about strategy. In the very short preface to the second edition (actually a re-issue) dated 2 September 1920, he berated Bogdanov, by now head of Proletkult, blaming him for introducing the bourgeois ideas.

The re-publication did not end the debate, or silence the opposition. On 8 October 1920 Lenin felt compelled to draw up a hasty outline for a Resolution, insisting that it be submitted 'this very day to the People's Commissariat of Education and to the "Proletkult" Congress because today is the last day of their session'.[21] He deduced from a report in *Izvestia* that Lunacharsky, as head of Narkompros, had been treading dangerously close to Bogdanov's heretical line on proletarian culture. There were major differences between Bogdanov's view—that pre-revolutionary culture had

nothing to offer to proletarian culture, not to mention those of his associates whose extremism on the matter included destroying all pre-revolutionary
art—and that of the culturally conservative Lenin. Other points also made
him uncomfortable. For instance, Bogdanov and Lunacharsky chose to
appoint associates from their years abroad as fellow members of their
respective organisations; furthermore the Proletkult had been established as
an effective body in July 1917, *before* Lenin's October cabinet (Sovnarkom).

In 1918, Bogdanov had proposed 'close collaboration' as the means by
which the proletariat would reject the 'spirit of subordination to the regime
of the ruling class' implicit in the old art.[22] On one level it was this rejection of the pre-revolutionary cultural heritage for which Lenin castigated
Bogdanov. Ultimately, though, the chink left for autonomy in Bogdanov's
cherished belief that art will fuse with working life and that 'collectivism illu-
minates the depiction not only of human life, but also of the life of nature',
which he affirmed in 1920, was incompatible with Lenin's *realpolitik*.[23]

Lunacharsky was trying desperately to tread a middle line between the
emphases of Bogdanov and of Lenin with respect to the old and the new
in art at that time. Lenin had long believed that unregulated artistic expression would prejudice the attainment of socialism: 'This absolute freedom
is a bourgeois or an anarchist phrase (since, as a world outlook, anarchism
is bourgeois philosophy turned inside out). One cannot live in society and
be free from society. The freedom of the bourgeois...artist is simply
masked dependence...on the money-bag'. In any case, a non-class art 'will
be possible only in a socialist extra-class society', meanwhile remaining
'*openly* linked to the proletariat'. It is the *openness* that is at the heart here.
Lenin's essay, first published in 1905 in *Novaya Zhizn*, warned of the
inevitability, 'now that we are becoming a mass party, changing abruptly to
an open organisation...that we shall be joined by many who are inconsis-
tent...and even by some mystics'.[24]

A fear of mysticism was indeed part of Lenin's attack on idealism, but
this was coupled with a theoretical repudiation of the idea that cultural
change should proceed relatively independently through adult education and
the promotion of the cultural development. For Lenin, by and large, the 'cultural question' would be resolved through the revolutionary struggle within
a new dispensation in the relations of production and the radical realignment of class rule. By 1920 Proletkult had grown vigorously, with support
from trade unions, factory committees and soviets. Much energy was
devoted to the organisation of libraries and classes and a large proportion
of its admittedly small budget was devoted to promoting drama and theatre
for working-class audiences. Bogdanov's ideas, notably that cultural activi-

ties at all levels were part of the class struggle in themselves, were coming to be widely discussed and somewhat influential even at high levels within the Bolshevik party. Furthermore, many left-wing political tendencies were at work within it, obviously including Mensheviks among others. The dispute was of long standing and had involved all the myriad opinions that make writing about this period so difficult to condense. What is more, the all-out struggle to suppress anarchism had not yet been engaged. We will restrict ourselves to saying that many of Proletkult's adult education activities were taken over by Narkompros, obviously including political education, and it was decided also that its activities in the arts should be monitored by the Communist party. In these respects its autonomy was curtailed although Lunacharsky struggled to keep the crucial issues of the cultural debate open.

The long-standing artistic isolation of Russia, by now part of the Soviet Union, began to ease for a few brief years after the close of the civil war and the rich creative developments that had occurred were communicated to the outside world. Kandinsky emigrated, joining the Bauhaus, his own proposals for art education having been rejected by his colleagues. Gabo and Pevsner also left, signalling that the rapid drive towards productivism could not easily accommodate the direction in which they believed constructivism might be taken. Chagall, ousted by Malevich from his position as head of the art school in Vitebsk in 1917, went too. An exhibition of modern Russian art was shown at the Van Diemen Gallery in Berlin in 1922, including a variety of works from paintings to productivist artefacts, partly orchestrated by Lissitsky. It had a strong impact and was received in the West as a powerful new form of art emerging from a new society. Meanwhile, back in the Soviet Union, the days of the *avant-garde* as an independent, controversial and socially critical movement were clearly numbered. Great achievements were still in store, particularly in film, in architecture and in theatre. And it was possible for many individuals to subsist within art schools and as teachers in the fields of design and experiment. But the Russian *avant-garde*, having passed from being scornful critics of autocracy, through a brief period when they saw themselves collectively as being at one with the revolution and the future, were no longer viewed in their homeland as the 'leading wave' but became subservient to Party expediency.

Thus it is indeed an irony that pioneers of twentieth-century art and creativity should have so affected both Tsarist and Soviet governments. The obscenity trial to which Goncharova was subjected hinged ultimately on the charge that her hedonistic materialism was undermining the spiritual order to which Mother Russia was consecrated. It was the allegedly idealist and mystical leanings of her generation of artists that Narkompros distrusted and was so determined to control. As a sub-culture the art of the *avant-garde* was an irritant and seen as a subversion by two radically opposed regimes.

Notes

1. St Petersburg was known as Petrograd between 1914 and 1924 and Leningrad thereafter. For simplicity we have settled on 'Petersburg' throughout.
2. Mikhail Larionov and Natalya Goncharova, 'Rayonists and Futurists. A manifesto' (1913) in John Bowlt (ed. and transl.), *Russian Art of the Avant-Garde. Theory and criticism 1902–1934* (London, 1976), pp.89–91.
3. Naum Gabo and Anton Pevsner, 'The realist manifesto' (1920) in Bowlt, *Russian Art*, pp.209–214.
4. Vasilly Kandinsky, 'Concerning the spiritual in art', in Charles Harrison and Paul Wood (eds), *Art in Theory, 1900–1990. An anthology of changing ideas* (Oxford, 1992), p.87.
5. N. G. Chernishevsky published *The Aesthetic Relation of Art to Reality* in 1855 and the utopian novel *What Is To Be Done* in 1863.
6. Bowlt, *Russian Art*, p.xxxvii.
7. Bowlt, *Russian Art*, p.78.
8. Camilla Gray, *The Russian Experiment in Art 1863–1922* (London, 1986), p.155.
9. Umbro Appolonio (ed.), *Futurist Manifestos* (London, 1970), pp.49–50 (italics in the original). The other authors of the catalogue statement were Carlo Carra, Luigi Russolo, Giacomo Balla and Gino Severini.
10. Bowlt, *Russian Art*, pp.144–5.
11. 'Those real Amazons, those Scythian riders', in the Futurist poet Benedict Livshit's words.
12. Serge Fauchereau (ed.), *Moscow: 1900–1930* (London, 1988), p.84.
13. 'A slap in the face of public taste' was the title of a collection of manifestos published by a group of Futurist writers in 1912.
14. Cited in Stanislas Zadora, 'The arts after the Revolution, 1917–1930' in Fauchereau, *Moscow 1900–1930* (London, 1988), p.89.
15. Tatlin was Director of the Department of Fine Arts (IZO). He wrote a 'Memorandum of the Moscow Artistic Collegium of the People's Commissariat of Education to the Council of People's Commissars, on the erection in Moscow of 50 monuments to outstanding figures in the area of revolutionary and social activity, in philosophy, literature, sciences and the arts' in June 1918. This is one of the basic documents which define the tasks and manner of organisation of the 'plan for monumental propaganda' put forward by Lenin in the spring of 1918. Tatlin's Letter to Lunacharsky was written sometime between 18 September and 10 October 1918. See L. Zhadova, *Tatlin*, (Hungary, 1984 and London, 1988), pp.186, 188.
16. Vladimir Mayakovsky, 'How to make verses', in Catriona Kelly (ed.), *Utopias. Russian modernist texts 1905–1940* (Harmondsworth, 1997), p.92.

17. Prouns, an acronym for 'Projects for the affirmation of the new', were an intermediate point between basic two- dimensional suprematist schemes and three-dimensional architectural schemes, designed by Lissitsky as 'a station on the way to constructing a new form'.

18. For different emphases on this debate, see for example: Gray, *Russian Experiment*; Sheila Fitzpatrick, *The Commissariat of Enlightenment. Soviet organisation of education and the arts under Lunacharsky, October 1917–1921* (Cambridge, 1970); A. Gleason et al. (eds), *Bolshevik Culture* (Bloomington, 1985); B. Taylor, *Art and Literature under the Bolsheviks. The crisis of renewal* (London, 1991).

19. Cited in Zadora, 'The Arts', p.95.

20. 'Fideism' is a doctrine which substitutes faith for knowledge, or which generally attaches significance to faith' (Lenin, *Materialism and Empirio-Criticism*, footnote to preface of first edition, September 1908).

21. Lenin's notes for the resolution cited in the catalogue to the Hayward Gallery exhibition *Art in Revolution. Soviet art and design since 1917* (London, 1971), p.17.

22. Alexander Bogdanov, 'The proletarian and art' (1918) in Bowlt, *Russian Art*, p.177.

23. Alexander Bogdanov, 'The paths of proletarian creation' (1920) in Bowlt, *Russian Art*, p.181.

24. V. I. Lenin, 'Party organization and party literature' (November 1905) in *Selected Works* (Moscow, 1968), p.151. Italics in the original.

For a Proletarian Culture
Communist Party culture in Britain in the Third Period, 1928–1935

Matthew Worley

The cultural history of the Communist Party of Great Britain (CPGB) has attracted significant interest over the past twenty years.[1] Seminal works by Alun Howkins, Stephen Jones, Raphael Samuel, Bert Hogenkamp and, more recently, Andy Croft, have unveiled a veritable secret history of communist-inspired activity ranging from workers' film, theatre and sporting groups, to literary ventures that exerted an influence way beyond the Party's relatively limited boundaries.[2] The CPGB has, quite rightly, been seen to have forged distinctly working-class cultural initiatives, injecting a Bolshevik rigour into such activity that contrasted noticeably with other sections of the British labour movement. This was particularly evident during the so-called Third Period—officially 1928 to 1935—during which time the CPGB endeavoured to construct an independent leadership of the working class in opposition to the Labour Party and trade union bureaucracy.[3] Consequently, as Alun Howkins has suggested, '[the] political break with social democracy forced a cultural break' as the Communist Party strove to delineate educational, creative and artistic alternatives to both bourgeois and labour-socialist norms.[4] This article will endeavour to outline the emergence of this distinctly proletarian culture before assessing the effectiveness of key CPGB initiatives.

Towards a revolutionary alternative

The cultural activities of the CPGB in the years immediately following its conception in 1920 related both to the means by which the party was created—through a fusion of existing socialist organisations—and to the party's initial strategy of working within the established British labour movement. Communists either retained their membership and/or commitment to existing institutions (the Plebs League, Labour Colleges); participated in grassroots movements (Socialist Sunday Schools); or became members of newly formed organisations such as the British Workers' Sports Federation

(BWSF), London Film Society or Workers' Theatre Movement (WTM).[5] By
the end of the decade however, the party had established numerous alternative cultural organisations, including party schools, rambling clubs and film
societies, and, in the case of both the BWSF and WTM, gained full practical and ideological control of previously diffuse labour initiatives. By 1929,
party members across the country were encouraged to develop 'new methods of working-class sociability and entertainment' and, in the midst of what
is generally regarded as a period of Communist Party decline, local comrades
forged a vibrant cultural environment based upon communist perceptions
and principles.[6]

The development of a distinctly communist working-class culture was a
by-product of several inter-linking factors. As Howkins and Jones have
demonstrated, the theoretical basis of the Third Period was fundamental to
the party's withdrawal from, and dismissal of, established cultural organisations and practice.[7] In a period of intensifying class struggle, wherein the
forces of social democracy were reportedly aligned with capital *against* the
workers, 'old' forms of working-class culture were dismissed as 'ideological
weapons of the bourgeoisie'—and thus inimical to the interests of the working class.[8] Consequently, comrades such as Tom Thomas, Jimmy Miller
(Ewan MacColl), George Sinfield, Michael Condon, Ralph Bond and Charlie
Mann endeavoured to formulate cultural practice that stood apart, and in
opposition to, existing cultural norms. Most obviously, the WTM devised an
agit-prop theatre that could be performed on street corners, the back of a
lorry or in the midst of 'the struggle'. Stage, curtain and props were discarded
in preference to multi-disciplined, collectively written sketches that sought
to incorporate the audience within the performance and which could be
adapted to relate directly to the workers' environment (*Rail Revolt, The P.A.C.
Sketch, Murder in the Coalfield*). Where capitalist theatre 'served to blind the
workers to the existence of the class struggle', and Labour/ILP theatre
attempted to bring 'capitalist art' to the workers or dealt merely 'with the
misery of the workers', the WTM, in contrast, 'unmask[ed] the capitalist system' while simultaneously 'organs[ing] the workers to fight their way out'.[9]

Similarly, the BWSF and the Federation of Workers' Film Societies (the
latter was established in October 1929) formulated overtly political consti-
tutions that encompassed the 'new line' of the CPGB.[10] Communist
domination of the BWSF revolved around Walter Tapsell's successful resolution that the federation unleash an 'unrelenting struggle against the
existing capitalist domination of sport' and, in the wake of communist ascendancy to local and national federation executives, broadsides against
professional sport (a 'dope to distract the workers') and such 'social fascist'

organisations as the labour-socialist National Workers' Sports Association (NWSA) were regularly issued by the party press.[11] In the process, the TUC, Clarion Cycling Club and Labour Party withdrew their support, leaving the CPGB to 'direct the instinct for sport on the part of the workers into channels that serve their own interests on the sports field, and in the field of industry'.[12] As such, the BWSF not only organised sports clubs, events and competitions, but also instigated campaigns in favour of better municipal facilities for local sports people while adroitly linking the lack of workers'-playing fields, leisure time and amenities to the perceived capitalist offensive against the working class.[13]

The Federation of Workers' Film Societies (FWFS) meanwhile, resolved to produce, distribute and show films 'of value to the working class'.[14] The Atlas film company was established to supply Soviet and German films to the numerous societies that had emerged prior to, and in the wake of, the FWFS' formation.[15] Moreover, a series of *Workers Topical News* was produced in 1930–32 to counter the 'capitalist propaganda' of mainstream newsreels, recording significant events in the workers' struggle such as unemployed marches, industrial disputes, May Day celebrations and demonstrations against imperialism. In line with the BWSF and WTM, the FWFS resolved to utilise film as yet another 'weapon in the struggle', developing 'revolutionary' techniques and theories that combated capitalist cinema's attempt to 'dope the workers'.[16] The 'natural conditions' of FWFS films and the rejection of either sets or actors was celebrated by the party, while productions such as *1931—The Charter Film* endeavoured to show not only the 'contradictions of capitalism', but also, in the form of workers in the midst of struggle, the revolutionary way out.

However, while the 'new line' offered theoretical justification for 'independent' and innovative communist initiative, it would be wrong to assume that the policies of the Third Period marked the beginning of the CPGB's divorce from the wider labour movement. Rather, the new line was, in part, a product of hardening ideological divisions evident within all areas of the British labour movement prior to the party's adoption of 'Class against Class' in 1928. In more orthodox political and industrial spheres for example, Labour Party and TUC measures against communist agitation within their respective ranks had intensified in the immediate wake of the 1926 General Strike, as tensions inherent in the party's united front policy came to the fore. Similarly, ideological and practical disparities were also apparent in the labour movement's more cultural auxiliaries prior to 1928. The party had already severed its links with the Plebs League by 1923, seceded from the Socialist Sunday Schools by 1924, and provoked acute ideological fissures in the

Labour College Movement by 1926, wherein communist criticism of the college syllabus, and the reciprocal anti-communism of the National Council of Labour Colleges (NCLC) Secretary, J.P.M. Millar, led to the expulsion of communist students between 1926 and 1929.[17]

In a number of instances, party members pre-empted the independent line of 'Class against Class'. The disputes that finally split the BWSF in 1928, for instance, had begun well before the CPGB's adoption of the new line in the same year. The prominent role communists such as Sinfield, Condon and Walter Tapsell played within the federation; the symbolism placed upon a 1927 football tour of the Soviet Union and the overtly political objectives proposed by Sinfield in his pamphlet *The Workers' Sports Movement* (1927); and the London section's decision to send a delegate to the tenth anniversary of the Bolshevik revolution against the wishes of the federation leadership, had already caused the BWSF executive to fear the '[violation] of the spirit of TUC and Labour Party support' by October 1927.[18] The new line merely compounded this emergent divide.

Concurrently, as Raphael Samuel has recognised, the 'rise and extension of the Workers' Theatre Movement was closely associated with, *and anticipated*, the "left" turn' of the CPGB.[19] The WTM had emerged out of the obscure Council for Proletarian Art in 1926 and initially received the support of ILP branches, the Plebs League, the Central Labour College and the *Daily Herald*.[20] However, debate over the content and direction of the movement, and the party's encroaching ideological and practical domination, soon eroded whatever links the wider labour movement wished to have with the WTM. As early as 1926, Huntley Carter outlined the WTM's policy of 'direct action', describing the movement as a 'propaganda machine' grounded in the class struggle and focused on topical issues relevant to the working class. Similarly, the agit-prop methods that later characterised the WTM were also referred to prior to the adoption of the new line in 1928, while the limitations of 'reformist', or rather non-communist, drama were regularly defined within the party press.[21] Despite such 'fumbling towards the idea of an agit-prop theatre' however, it was undoubtedly the ideological tenets of the new line that augmented the WTM's transformation into a 'propertyless theatre for a propertyless class'.[22]

Alternative, distinctly communist, educational structures had also been established prior to the party's adoption of 'Class against Class'. Party training groups were initiated as part of the CPGB's 'Bolshevisation' from 1922, although it was not until late 1924, following Comintern criticism of Party education at the Fifth Congress of the Communist International, that Tom Bell devised a party training manual for local and district groups, and

October 1926 before a Central Party Training School was established in London.[23] Consequently, a syllabus in keeping with the Bolshevik perspective was developed, focusing on party structure and organisation as well as political and economic theory. Furthermore, the party endeavoured to formulate 'alternative' teaching methods, with Bell's revised training manual of 1927 instructing Party trainers not to be 'a lecturer showing his knowledge', but a tutor who 'asks questions [and] provokes discussion'.[24] Indeed, following the adoption of the new line, the Party sought to replace the lecture method completely, and a programme of 'collective reports' was developed based upon 'different comrades [paying] attention to special points'. Learning became a 'collective responsibility' with the party committed to ensuring a 'Leninist education' for all its members.[25]

The influence of both the Comintern and the Soviet Union was fundamental to the CPGB's cultural development, and this was perhaps most evident within the educational sphere. Not only was the party syllabus based increasingly upon the Comintern line but the establishment in 1924 of the Lenin School in Moscow gave the CPGB an illustrious alternative to the NCLC based at the heart of the revolution. Although the first British delegation to the school in 1926 had been critical of the extensive study programme—so much so that the Comintern threatened to send the British students home—Lenin School graduates became integral to the dissemination of 'correct' party policy and strategy.[26] And while study in Moscow undoubtedly raised the level of Marxist understanding among communists in Britain, the doctrinaire approach to Marxist-Leninist theory, the Comintern jargon, and the very evident veneration of the USSR, compounded the extraneous character of the CPGB and arguably hindered the emergence of any truly original thinkers within the party.[27]

The influence of the USSR was evident in other ways. The showing of Soviet films was central to the FWFS, Soviet songs were often sung at party events, the WTM was undoubtedly influenced by the revolutionary theatre in Russia (as Raphael Samuel has made clear), and deference to the first workers' state was prevalent throughout the party press.[28] However, while it would be historically naive to deny the importance of the Soviet example to the CPGB, the party was also influenced by international and indigenous factors. Links with the German communist movement, for example, were integral to the development of the WTM's agit-prop style. Tom Thomas had been profoundly affected by his trip to the Ruhr in the Spring of 1930, and German comrades frequently visited Britain to offer advice to fledgling theatre groups.[29] Similarly, the dungarees of the Salford Red Megaphones replicated the uniform of the German theatre groups, and Jimmy Miller's regular correspondence with Rudi Lehmann alerted the Manchester communist to the scripts, scores and methods of his German contemporaries.[30] Moreover, indigenous influences remained embedded in CPGB culture. The particular focus of party culture on football, cycling, rambling, theatre and even film—and the fastidiousness of the CPGB's approach to education— had clear British precedents, while the deliberate application of cultural initiatives to existing 'struggles' necessitated an awareness of local conditions and perspectives.

Overall therefore, the CPGB's development of a 'proletarian culture' evolved out of the complex interaction of national and international forces. On one level, the party's cultural activities, like the party itself, emerged from existing labour movement structures and adhered to traditions inherent in British working-class history. On another level, the CPGB was infused with a revolutionary fervour, coloured by the tenets of Bolshevism, that profoundly influenced its development (politically and culturally) and distinguished communist activity from that of the wider British labour movement. For members of the CPGB, the personal, political and cultural flowed together to form a totality that ensured that cultural activity was yet another realm of the class conflict in which a 'relentless struggle' had to be fought. For this reason, the cultural initiatives of the CPGB throughout the Third Period resonated an inventiveness and vigour that contrasted with parallel labour-socialist organisations such as the NWSA or the Masses Stage and Film Guild.[31]

The British Workers' Sports Federation

In the wake of the CPGB's successful usurpation of the BWSF administration, the Clarion Cycling Club, TUC and Labour Party all withdrew their support and thereby left the party in a position to fundamentally realign the federation's objectives and perspectives. Thus, affiliation to the Lucerne Sports International was replaced by affiliation to the Comintern's Red Sports International (RSI) and the activities of the federation became more politicised and widespread. At a grassroots level, the party's request for comrades to develop and extend local sporting groups met with an enthusiastic response, as new branches emerged across the country and a wide variety of activity was instigated. Indeed, Glasgow alone had six BWSF sections representing over 400 members in 1930, and by June 1931 the federation claimed to represent some 6,000 members.[32]

Cycling was particularly popular as Red Wheelers formed in Rochdale, Eastwood, Leeds, Doncaster and most other party localities, and a regular cycle ride from London to Brighton was organised in the South East. Boxing, football and rambling were the other principal sporting favourites. In Newcastle, a boxing gym of 60 members was established in 1930 and tournaments were regularly held in South Wales, Manchester and Scotland. Football leagues emerged in Fife, London, South Wales and Derby, and Sunday rambles became a customary fixture for most BWSF branches. Elsewhere, local organisations responded to the demands or sporting inclinations of their members and subsequently BWSF cricket matches were played in Bradford, a workers' hockey team was formed in Shipley, a workers' tennis club emerged on Tyneside, and a baseball team was developed in the Rhondda![33]

The London branches were particularly active—due to the close proximity of a number of clubs and their nearness to the federation centre—and London-wide competitions ranging from swimming galas and football leagues to netball championships were organised. (Fifty teams competed for the latter in 1932, with the trophy eventually being won by the Fairclough team.) In Manchester, meanwhile, the Workers' Arts Club housed a boxing gym, while the local BWSF organised regular, well-attended Sunday rambles and cycling trips. Camping jaunts were also arranged, such as that to Clough Head Farm in 1932, where in spite of logistical problems—and 'E.F's' [Eddie Frow's?] insistence that he took a typewriter, Lenin's collected works and six volumes of *Inprecorr*—180 comrades enjoyed a good-humoured weekend of singing, discussion and rambling.[34] Most famously, the Lancashire branches of the BWSF (led by Benny Rothman) formed the Ramblers' Rights Movement through which the mass trespass at Kinder Scout in April 1932 was organised.[35]

Indeed, politics were invariably incorporated into BWSF activity. In Tottenham, the local BWSF launched a successful campaign against the local council's 'No Sunday Games' policy in 1930, and in 1931 a London Workers' Football Council (with 99 affiliated clubs) was organised to give assistance to workers' teams, to form football leagues, and to campaign for better facilities and Sunday sports. Elsewhere, campaigns for worker access to municipal amenities were organised in Hackney, Stepney and Hampstead, and such activity gained considerable support amongst local workers, sports people and from trade union branches.[36] More radically, BWSF cyclists in Leeds volunteered their services to the plight of the unemployed, rallying 400 workers to prevent bailiffs evicting working-class victims of the means test.[37] And in an industrial context, BWSF members repeatedly involved themselves in workers' strike action, organising football matches and raising strike funds.[38] As such, workers' sport was intended to facilitate class consciousness, with

Harry Pollitt (the BWSF President) venturing that by appealing to 'young workers interested in swimming and football, the Party could generate an interest in the unemployed workers and so on'.[39] However, more general political campaigns, such as the CPGB/BWSF call for workers to boycott a 1930 Sixth Round FA Cup tie at West Ham's Upton Park in protest against the high admission prices, proved futile. As the *Daily Worker* acknowledged, a 'huge crowd' attended.[40]

Centrally, a number of initiatives, not all of them successful, were instigated by the BWSF executive. A women's section was established in early 1930 to complement the federation's commitment to 'women's sport', and although the CPGB was not 'progressive' enough to see far beyond netball and gym classes, the intention was to encourage female participation in athletics, rambling and cycling. Moreover, national and international events were entered and organised by the federation. Worker teams regularly visited Europe and the USSR, such as in April 1932 when 36 delegates of the BWSF spent two months in Russia to participate in athletics, boxing, cycling and swimming tournaments. Similarly, the BWSF competed in the Soviet Spartakiades of 1928 and 1932, and various tours of Germany, France, Norway and Switzerland were undertaken. In return, French and German workers visited Britain, while a proposed Russian football tour of the UK in 1930 was famously blighted by the Labour foreign secretary's [J.R. Clynes's] refusal to submit visas to the Russian team. Even so, a number of projected excursions were also cancelled due to financial and logistical restraints. Money was a constant cause of consternation for the executive, and getting time off work could prove difficult for participants.[41]

More successful was the Red Sports Day organised by the BWSF. On 25 April 1930, 1,000 spectators watched a plethora of sporting events in Hyde Park, at which the West Ham ILP Guild of Youth won the *Daily Worker* football trophy and Hackney Girls won the netball cup.[42] Successful inter-regional football matches, boxing tournaments and cycling tours were also undertaken between 1928 and 1933. One football match between London and South Wales workers was watched by a crowd of over 3,000 for example; and a London swimming gala, held at Haggerston Baths in 1930, was later described as 'the best organised and most successful sporting event held by the BWSF'.[43]

Ultimately however, the BWSF remained a marginal organisation. Financial and organisational problems continually haunted the federation, and although its achievements were significant, the importance of the BWSF was more regional and social than national. Even so, the commitment of its members encapsulated the spirit of the CPGB and thereby provided entertainment, excursions and activity to thousands of workers both in and out of the party.[44] In terms of football alone, the BWSF claimed to represent some 5,000 players in 1931.[45] Furthermore, through its trips abroad the federation offered workers the opportunity to visit and perform in places beyond the reach of the average working-class wage packet,[46] while the local campaigns for free municipal amenities and rambling rights had a resonance that extended far beyond communist circles. Indeed, the reputation of the federation was such that by 1932 many Clarion Cycling Clubs and ILP branches were applying to (re-)affiliate to the BWSF.[47] While not constituting a conspicuous alternative to 'professional' or 'capitalist' sport therefore, the BWSF was distinctly working class in its basis and outlook, and constituted a remarkable expression of British communist initiative and dedication.

The Workers' Theatre Movement

The Workers' Theatre Movement was the most innovative and radical of the CPGB's cultural auxiliaries in the Third Period. It sought not merely to utilise theatre as a propaganda weapon but to radically transform the very nature of theatrical production, overhauling both the methods of presentation and the space in which sketches were performed. As outlined above, this was facilitated by both new line attempts to divorce communist activity from that of the bourgeois and labour-socialist, and by a conscious effort to give workers' theatre a revolutionary quality—a role in 'the struggle'. As Jimmy Miller later complained, WTM performances had originally taken place in local trade union or Co-op halls where 'everybody knew each other—it was an audience of maybe twenty, twenty five people. And there I was wanting to see the revolution!'[48] Moreover, despite the radical intentions of the original WTM, its patronage of worker-playwrights such as the Scottish miner Jim Corrie, and the working-class character of most local workers' theatre groups, the central organisation was dominated by those Raphael Samuel has described as 'upper-middle class bohemians' (Huntley Carter, Christina Walshe, Havelock Ellis) who appeared as interested in modernist aesthetics as the social revolution.[49] It was such 'inadequacies' that provided the impetus for the revolutionary agit-prop theatre of 1930–35.

The publication of the *Daily Worker* from 1 January 1930 further facilitated the WTM's development and transformation, and articles encouraging worker correspondents to report on the activities of local theatre groups were evident from the outset. Tom Thomas, who emerged as the leading figure in the WTM, had a weekly column, and it was on 10 May 1930, after his witnessing the Workers' Theatre League in the Ruhr, that Thomas outlined the 'new tactics' of the WTM, calling on every local party branch to develop a theatre group to produce 'popular and direct' sketches that could be performed in the 'open air or on a lorry'. In particular, Thomas advised, popular songs should be parodied (*Sonny Boy* became *Money Boy*) and conventional stage sets, naturalistic settings, props and curtains should be discarded.[50]

The consequences of this realignment were soon evident. By 1931, ten workers' theatre groups existed in London alone, including the Red Star Troupe of West London, Red Radio of Hackney, the Red Magnets of Woolwich, the Red Front of Streatham, the Red Players of Lewisham, the Red Blouses of Greenwich and the Yiddish-speaking Proletet based in the East End.[51] Elsewhere, the Dundee Red Front Troupe, the Edinburgh Red Pioneers, the Liverpool Red Anchors and the Sunderland Red Magnets affiliated to the WTM, while a weekend school for fledgling theatre groups based in the North and the Midlands attracted 40 delegates from eight towns in May 1931.[52] By the first National Conference of the WTM, held in London's Cromer Street on 25–26 June 1932, some 30 groups were estimated to have 'been at work'.[53] In the meantime, explicitly political scripts, focusing on local (*The Market Quack in Hackney*), national (*Doctor Mac*, about Ramsay MacDonald's 'cures' for unemployment) and international (*Meerut*) issues, were disseminated among the various troupes as the WTM became an increasingly prevalent form of communist agitation. Theatre groups regularly accompanied party speakers, agitated in election campaigns (performing such plays as *The Crisis* and *Jimmy Maxton and the I.L.P.* in 1931), and entertained comrades at party socials, festivals and events.

In Lancashire, the Salford Red Megaphones exemplified the new spirit of the WTM. Based around the nucleus of Miller, Joe Davies, Grace Sodden, Alex Armstrong, Len Heckert, Flo Clayton, Nellie Wallace and Martin Bobker, the Megaphones developed a series of collectively written scripts which they performed across the region. Dressed in dungarees (in the style of their German comrades), the group appeared outside factory gates, at local labour exchanges and on the backs of trucks, performing in the midst of unemployed demonstrations and in the textile towns at the centre of the 'more looms' dispute of 1931–32. Their scripts included *The P.A.C. Sketch, The Trial of Private Enterprise* and numerous songs and skits written in relation to the Lancashire workers' struggle.[54] Such pieces were further adapted to fit specific local conditions, taking into account the numerous working methods and labour divisions of the textile industry, and were intended to 'rouse our audiences to immediate action [with] words that would burn like fire and set our slums ablaze'.[55]

In such a way, the WTM acutely fused the cultural and the political. The movement's journal, *The Red Stage* (edited by Charlie Mann), consistently defined the revolutionary perspective of the WTM, while the first National Conference detailed the advantages of an agit-prop style that was flexible and adaptable, prioritised the 'actor's' class experience (over technical ability) and took place amongst the working class.[56] And although we must retain our perspective—most WTM troupes consisted of only a handful of members—the movement encapsulated the total world of the CPGB and thus produced a truly working-class theatre rooted firmly in the class struggle.

The Workers' Film Society

Although the propaganda value of film was recognised by the wider labour movement in the 1920s, several logistical problems hampered the development of an effective labour, or working-class, film movement. Subsequently, while communist-inspired initiatives often fared better than their labour-socialist 'competitors', the various Workers' Film Societies of the Third Period cannot be regarded as so successful an expression of 'proletarian culture' as either the BWSF or the WTM.[57]

First, the cost of film projection and production was not cheap, and the initial formation of specifically *working-class* film societies was actually prompted, in part, by the high subscription rates of, for example, the London Film Society (25 shillings).[58] However, although the FWFS attempted to rectify this, members and potential members remained critical of subscription rates/prices that fared unfavourably with commercial cinema.[59] Similarly, the equipment both to show and produce films was costly. The London WFS had only one portable projector, and *1931—The Charter Film*, despite being made on a low-cost budget of £50, was still a relatively expensive production for an organisation that would record a loss of £500 by December 1931.

Second, censorship by both the British Board of Film Censors (BBFC) and local authorities consistently hampered the fledgling film groups. The first London performance following the establishment of the FWFS was delayed as a result of London County Council (LCC) intervention, for example; the Salford Watch Committee prohibited the Salford WFS from showing the Soviet-made *Storm over Asia* (Pudovkin) in May 1931, forcing the society to show the film 'over the border' in Manchester; the Glasgow Corporation continually blighted the local WFS' plans to show Soviet films; and on Merseyside, the activities of the WFS prompted condemnation in the local press, a ban on WFS film shows at the university hall, and the forced resignation of the society's secretary, a teacher, whose employers did not take kindly to such extra-curricular activity.[60] Although ways were found to defy such censorship, the history of every WFS is peppered with protracted battles against the municipal authorities.

Third, the unwieldy nature of film equipment meant that it was harder for the FWFS to 'go to the workers' in the way the WTM was able to. Technical knowledge and experience was needed, and although the various societies quickly came to terms with their equipment, problems still occurred (see below). As such, the WFS could afford to be neither a propertied nor a propertyless organisation and its impact on 'the struggle' was subsequently less evident. Although the WTM did attempt to project films directly onto the South London streets following the collapse of the FWFS in 1932, such experiments appear to have been short lived.[61]

Even so, these difficulties did not deter comrades such as Ralph Bond in London and Tom Cavanagh in Manchester from actively attempting to develop specifically working-class film shows, productions and distribution. Soviet films had previously been exhibited by CPGB auxiliary organisations (Friends of Soviet Russia, and Workers' International Relief), as well as by broader non-aligned organisations such as the London Film Society. With the formation of the FWFS in October 1929, and the simultaneous establishment of the Atlas film company, however, such activity gained an explicitly British political agenda (as outlined above). Moreover, the London Workers' Film Society did see an impressive increase in membership over the first year of its existence, with 1,200 members recorded by October 1930 and the establishment of links to both trade union activists and such proletarian organisations as the Association of Women Clerks and Secretaries.[62] Audience figures meanwhile depended on the venue and programme, but attendances in excess of 2,000 were recorded by the Daily Worker and societies occasionally succeeded in showing Soviet films at commercial cinemas.[63]

Across the country, the FWFS registered 3,000 members by late 1931 with functioning or provisional societies in London, Salford, Liverpool, Edinburgh, Glasgow, Newcastle, Derby, Middlesborough, Birmingham and Nottingham.[64] Soviet, Atlas and—for a little light relief—non-political films (Disney cartoons, 'cultural' films and comedies) were shown, with audiences again varying in size from place to place and in relation to venue and programme.[65] The Salford WFS, for instance, claimed an average attendance of around 450 in its 1930–31 season and boasted a membership of 350 by the 1931–32 season. The Liverpool WFS, meanwhile, recorded regular audiences of more than 500. In addition, such practical activity was supplemented by the FWFS summer school of 1931—arranged to delineate the theory and practice of the federation—and the organisation of lectures and demonstrations by local societies.[66]

In terms of film production and distribution, Atlas distributed some 24 Soviet films between 1929 and 1931 and produced four 'workers' newsreels' (*Workers' Topical News*) and two 'workers' films' (*1931—The Charter Film* and *Glimpses of Modern Russia*). The home-grown material related directly to the activities of the CPGB, juxtaposing the 'capitalist offensive' (rationalisation, poverty, unemployment) with workers' demonstrations and Communist Party speakers. In addition, the Salford WFS, with the support of the FWFS, documented the on-going textile dispute for the third *Workers' Topical News* in late 1931. The technical difficulties of the time can be adjudged, however, by the fact that the film actually caught fire on its premiere performance at the Hyndman Hall, Salford.[67] It was not until 1934 that further 'workers productions' emerged.

Despite such characteristic communist eagerness and ingenuity, both the FWFS and Atlas were crippled by financial and organisational strains in 1932, and the federation proved to be the least sustainable of the party's cultural auxiliaries in the Third Period.[68] Even so, some local societies persevered, including the Manchester and Salford WFS, while worker film groups continued to be established by local CPGB branches. In London, the WTM, encouraged by the International Workers' Theatre Olympiad of May 1933, took up the initiative, utilising film in WTM productions and establishing Kino, a production and distribution company. The latter produced another series of *Workers' Newsreels*, along with films centred upon the unemployed (*Bread, Hunger March*), and forged a successful distribution network (Kino Films Limited) that flourished in the Popular Front period (1935–39). As such, although the party once again fused cultural initiative with political struggle, and established a cultural auxiliary that was run, and was geared towards, the British working class, the FWFS itself remained a marginal and limited organisation.

Communist Party education

The establishment of a nationwide education network was yet another distinct feature of the CPGB's cultural activity in the Third Period. Although initial attempts at 'party training' had not proven wholly successful—two early training groups established by the St. Pancras Party local in May 1926 reported that none of their 24 students completed the course—by November 1930 the party had established 11 District Party Schools and 72 Workers' Study Circles, tutoring 192 and 794 workers respectively.[69] London boasted the most impressive figures, with 25 party trainers teaching 47 comrades in two District Schools, and 24 study circles comprising 210 workers,

60 of whom were non-party members. The Scottish District Party mean-while recorded 12 study circles with 145 students; and in Sheffield three Party Schools taught 42 party members. Even in areas where party membership was relatively low, the CPGB had established functioning training groups by 1930. In Manchester, where the party amounted to just 244 members in November 1930, 23 members attended the District School and 147 work-ers (57 of whom were non-party members) attended ten local study circles. Of the regional party centres, only Liverpool remained without a District Party School at this time.[70]

By 1931, despite a slight fall in the number of party members attending the District Schools (192 to 185), the number of Workers' Study Circles had increased from 72 to 74 to accommodate 868 students, of whom 221 were non-party members. In addition, a Summer School was added to the party's education network and 'better political understanding...more initiative...improved collective work...[and] new elements coming in' were positively recorded.[71] In the midst of the party's numerical decline between 1927 and 1931, therefore, the CPGB was still able to construct an expand-ing educational basis. Even so, the CPGB remained aware of its deficiencies, as new methods of 'collective learning' were devised (outlined above) and a greater emphasis on women's, factory workers' and young comrades' edu-cation was regularly encouraged.

While the party developed teaching methods conducive to effective learning, and insisted that its Summer Schools and Workers' Study Circles were open to both party and non-party workers alike, the substance of CPGB education was rooted firmly in the tenets of Bolshevism and the Comintern line. The 1931 Summer School, for example, organised by Jack Murphy and held at the Cober Hill guest house near Scarborough between 11 and 18 July, included a lecture programme that featured such topics as 'Our party and the present period', 'Fascism and social fascism' and 'The Five Year Plan and the internal struggles of the Communist Party of the Soviet Union'.[72] Similarly, training manuals issued by the party's Agit-Prop department as a guide for party trainers were dominated by such topics as 'the organisation and development of capitalism' and 'the tactics of the pro-letariat after the conquest of power'.[73] Consequently, historical materialism was increasingly substituted for Soviet, and indeed Stalinist, orthodoxy—a fact compounded by the education offered by the Lenin School in Moscow—and this undoubtedly limited the party's wider educational appeal.

Even so, the educational opportunities offered to British workers by the Communist Party can be included among the finest achievements of the CPGB. The party's commitment to education, discussion and personal research was exemplary, and such encouragement of working-class initiative allowed those neglected by the wider British schooling system the chance to learn and express themselves. The party, more than any other section of the British labour movement, continued the autodidactic tradition embedded in British working-class history, and the rich literary heritage of the CPGB was but just one consequence of this.[74]

A proletarian culture?

The extensive cultural activity of the CPGB in the Third Period was synonymous with the political perspective of 'Class against Class' and the party's evident variance from the mainstream labour movement. In particular, such a development encapsulated the totality of the communist experience in which party membership was not merely a case of lending support, but of shaping the future: of serving 'the cause'. Beyond the workshop, trade union, party and unemployed activity of the CPGB cadre, a glance through the *Daily Worker* reveals a world of party socials, fancy dress carnivals and countless benefit events held to raise money for innumerable causes. Moreover, in each party region, cultural initiatives peculiar to particular localities also developed, including worker orchestras, unemployed bands and even Esperanto clubs.[75] It was within such a world that the activity described above must be placed.

While not all of the cultural initiatives of the Third Period proved successful—the Workers' Camera League established in 1932 to provide photos for press and propaganda purposes made little headway before being incorporated into the Workers' Film and Photo League in November 1934—CPGB activity was significant both for its members' ingenuity and for its innovation. Not only did the party develop functioning organisations in the face of financial, numerical and logistical difficulties, but the concepts articulated by CPGB, and the WTM in particular, were artistically radical. Charlie Mann's projection of an unemployed march onto a WTM performance in Shoreditch Town Hall, for example, was unprecedented in Britain, and such invention, in the words of Bert Hogenkamp, 'must have been a startling experience to British audiences' at the time.[76] Perhaps more importantly, the CPGB injected its cultural work into the workers' daily experience, thereby fusing the cultural and the political to form a distinctly militant 'proletarian culture'. Even so, despite being born out of opposition to existing bourgeois and labour-socialist cultural forms, the FWFS, BWSF and WTM were not exclusively sectarian. The Salford WFS, for example, played down its CPGB connections, while ILP and Labour Party teams participated in BWSF activities. Indeed, where sectarianism was noted, it was generally condemned.[77]

Between 1933 and 1935 the Third Period gave way to what would eventually become the period of the Popular Front against fascism and war, in which the CPGB would once again attempt to align itself with the mainstream labour movement. Consequently, the cultural initiatives forged between 1928 and 1932 similarly evolved to complement the party's changing political perspective. In terms of the party's distinct cultural auxiliaries, the consequences of this were mixed. While the BWSF slowly dissolved and the WTM swapped its agit-prop innovation for more formal methods (before mutating into the successful Unity Theatre), the film movement flourished in the more conciliatory climate of 1935–39; the party's cultural basis widened to include such organisations as the Workers' Music League; and the party's literary credentials were acutely revealed by the formation of the British Section of the Writers' International and the *Left Review*. Even so, while the cultural activity of the CPGB went from strength to strength in the late 1930s and 1940s, the initiatives and innovations of the Third Period remain fundamental to the CPGB's cultural development. Organisations such as the WTM, BWSF and FWFS encapsulated the total world of the party and party members, and thereby forged a distinctly proletarian culture peculiar to the British Communist Party.

Notes

1. The term 'culture' is, of course, open to theoretical debate. For the purposes of this article I have interpreted the word to mean, first, creative activity that can be regarded or participated in collectively, and second, activity directed towards mental enhancement.

2. A. Howkins, 'Class against Class. The political culture of the Communist Party of Great Britain, 1930–35' in F. Gloversmith (ed.), *Class, Culture and Social Change. A new view of the 1930s* (Brighton, 1980); S.G. Jones, *Workers at Play. A social and economic history of leisure* (London, 1986); Jones, *The British Labour Movement and Film, 1918–1939* (London, 1987); Jones, 'Sport, politics and the labour movement. The British Workers' Sports Federation, 1923–35', *British Journal of Sports History*, vol. 2, no. 2 (1985); R. Samuel, E. MacColl and S. Cosgrove, *Theatres of the Left. Workers' theatre movements in Britain and America, 1890–1935* (London, 1984); R. Samuel, 'The lost world of British Communism', parts 1–3, *New Left Review* nos. 154, 156, 165 (1985–1987); B. Hogenkamp, *Deadly Parallels. Film and the left in Britain, 1929–39* (London, 1986); A. Croft, *Red Letter Days. British fiction in the 1930s* (London, 1990), A. Croft (ed.), *A Weapon in the Struggle. The cultural history of the Communist Party in Britain* (London, 1998). The latter includes essays by numerous historians concerning graphic art, cultural journals such as *Left Review*, *Our Time* and *Seven*, jazz clubs, classical composers and theory.

3. By 1928, the Communist International, of which the CPGB was a loyal sec-

tion, had recognised three periods of post-war struggle. The first, between 1917 and 1922–3, was a period of revolutionary upheaval, while the second, between 1923 and 1927, was one of 'capitalist stabilisation'. The Third Period therefore, was to herald a fresh round of crises and revolution, as the contradictions inherent in capitalism induced a 'capitalist offensive', unemployment, industrial rationalisation, working-class militancy and imperialist war.

4. Howkins, 'Class against Class', p.254.
5. S. Macintyre, *A Proletarian Science. Marxism in Britain, 1917–1933* (Cambridge, 1980); M. Docherty, *A Miner's Lass* (Preston, 1992).
6. *Programme of the Young Communist International* (CPGB archives, National Museum of Labour History: henceforth NMLH).
7. Howkins, 'Class against Class', p.254, and Jones, *Workers*, p.156.
8. J. Cohen, 'The Communist Party and the Young Communist League', *Communist Review*, February 1930.
9. 'The basis and development of the Workers' Theatre Movement', from the First National Conference of the WTM, Charter Hall, London, 25–26 June 1932, reprinted in *History Workshop Journal* no.4 (1977).
10. In September 1929 the CPGB resolved to develop a film company and established a committee that included Maurice Dobb, Emile Burns and R.W. Robson, the London District Secretary (CPGB Political Bureau minutes, 12 September 1929, Klugmann Papers, NMLH). The following month, the London Workers' Film Society formed the basis for the Federation of Workers' Film Societies, and the Atlas Film Company Limited was established. Through the Minority Movement [NMM], the London society mobilised a degree of trade union support, but the CPGB dominated the new organisation. Ralph Bond was secretary, while the leadership included Burns, Ivor Montagu and Harry Pollitt. See NMM Executive Bureau minutes, 22 November 1929 (Jack Tanner papers, Nuffield College, Oxford). The main shareholders of Atlas were Emile Burns, Ralph Bond, Joan Beauchamp and Herbert Ward.
11. *Report of the First National Conference of the BWSF* 28 April 1928 (NMLH); for examples, see *Daily Worker*, 12 February and 25 July 1930, 20 June 1931; R.P. Dutt, 'Sport and Our Daily', 21 January 1930 (Dutt Papers, British Library).
12. *National Congress of the British Workers' Sports Federation* 6–7 December 1930 (NMLH).
13. M. Condon, *The Fight For The Workers' Playing Fields* (London, 1932). For example, the BWSF instigated a successful campaign against the Tottenham District Council ban on Sunday sports activity.
14. 'Constitution of the Federation of Workers' Film Societies' in *The Worker*, 22 November 1929. The same resolution was adopted by Manchester and Salford Workers' Film Society in 1930. See *Constitution of the Manchester and Salford Workers' Film Society* (Working-Class Movement Library, Salford: henceforth WCML).
15. By the first annual conference of the federation in September 1930, groups existed in London, Liverpool, Cardiff, Bradford, Salford, Edinburgh and

Glasgow. See Hogenkamp, *Parallels*, p.51.

16. *Daily Worker*, 4 February 1930; see, e.g., 'The film is a weapon', Workers' Cinema, November 1931 (cited in Hogenkamp, *Parallels*, pp.60–1).

17. See S. Macintyre, *Proletarian Science*, pp.80–5 and R. Samuel, 'Staying Power: The lost world of British Communism, part two', *New Left Review*, March-April 1986.

18. BWSF National Executive minutes, 16 October 1927 (NMLH); G. Sinfield, *The Workers' Sports Movement* (London, 1927). Sinfield suggested the BWSF wage a 'bitter and relentless struggle against all types of capitalist sports organisations'. The reason for the BWSF's weakness in Britain, he reasoned, was because sport was dominated by the ruling class in the form of professional sport, factory clubs, through to the Boy Scouts and Church Lads Brigades. Tom Groom, the BWSF secretary, offered his resignation in October 1927, but was convinced to stay on. George Sinfield was elected secretary at the National Conference in January 1928.

19. R. Samuel, 'Theatre and socialism in Britain 1880–1935', in Samuel, MacColl and Cosgrove, *Theatres*, p.33 (my emphasis).

20. Several regional drama clubs also emerged at this time. A Workers' Arts Club was established by Larry Finlay in Salford, a Manchester workers' theatre group evolved out of the Levenshulme Labour College, and Tom Thomas formed the Hackney People's Players.

21. See *Sunday Worker*, 6 June, 18 July, 22 August and 30 October 1926. For criticism of ILP drama see *Labour Monthly*, August 1926.

22. T. Thomas, 'A propertyless theatre for a propertyless class', *History Workshop Journal*, Autumn 1977 pp.113–27.

23. Macintyre, *Proletarian Science*, pp.85–7; CPGB Ninth Congress, *Reports, Theses and Resolutions* (London, 1927) p.29.

24. *Communist Party Training* (revised edn, London, 1927).

25. See *Outlines For Students and Party Trainers* (London, 1931) and D.R., 'The present state of party education', *Communist Review*, January 1931. 'We have had some experiences where one comrade gets up and lectures for two or three hours and then sits down hoping everybody else has something to say. The results have always fallen short of expectations …'

26. J.T. Murphy to CPGB Political Bureau, 11 April 1927 (Klugmann Papers, NMLH).

27. Macintyre, *Proletarian Science*, pp.86–7.

28. Programme for St. Pancras LPC Social, 4 February 1928 (Pollard papers, Bodleian Library); *Six Soviet Songs* (London, 1929); Samuel, 'Theatre', pp.42–43.

29. Tom Thomas, 'The workers' theatre of struggle', *Daily Worker*, 10 May 1930; *Daily Worker*, 11 June 1930, 3 January 1931.

30. E. MacColl, 'Theatre of action, Manchester', in Samuel, MacColl and Cosgrove, *Theatres*, p.229. A Comintern representative in Britain, 'Kitty' or 'Comrade Ludmilla', first introduced Miller to the notion of 'agit prop'.

31. According to Stephen Jones, 'not only did the MFSG fail to embark on any production initiatives of its own, but was also fairly inactive in film distribution'.

See Jones, *Film*, p.142. The Labour Party bureaucracy, meanwhile, remained suspicious of film societies in general. Nor did 'rival' organisations endeavour to cultivate radically new methods of theatre, film or education.

32. BWSF National Committee minutes, 7 June 1931 (NMLH). However, the membership of the various BWSF branches varied across the country and oscillated wildly. In 1932, the BWSF reported that the Bradford BWSF numbered 150, the Kirkcaldy (Fife) BWSF 100, Gateshead 160 and Hackney 170 (*Sports and Games*, October-November 1932).

33. These details are taken from various BWSF National and Sub Committee minutes held in the NMLH. The Welsh football league was forced to close in 1931, following the Rhondda District Council's ruling that teams playing in the BWSF league would not be allowed to play in the Rhondda League.

34. *BWSF Camp Souvenir* (NMLH).

35. *Daily Sketch*, 25 April 1932.

36. Condon, *Playing Fields*. The Stepney campaign succeeded in securing free access to a gym and netball pitches; BWSF National Committee minutes, 19 September 1930 (NMLH).

37. *Sports and Games*, January 1932.

38. Three examples were during the Yorkshire Woollen strike of 1930 and the Lancashire textile and London Lightermen strikes of 1932. See *Daily Worker*, 14 May 1930 and 29 January 1932. Also, *Report of the Third National Conference of the BWSF*, 4–5 March 1933 (WCML). At Burnley, during the Lancashire textile dispute of 1931, the BWSF organised a football match between two teams of strikers after which workers were rallied for a mass picket of a local mill. See Condon, *Playing Fields*.

39. CPGB Central Committee minutes, 13–14 August 1930 (NMLH).

40. *Daily Worker*, 1 and 4 March 1930.

41. By 1931, the BWSF's affiliation to the RSI was still due, the executive regularly discussed the difficulty of hiring facilities, grounds and equipment, and the federation's newspaper, *Worker Sportsman*, had long since collapsed. BWSF sub-committee minutes, 25 October 1928 (NMLH).

42. *Daily Worker*, 28 April 1930. BWSF Sub Committee minutes, 2 May 1930 (NMLH). Amusingly, the *Daily Worker* missed out the 'ILP' part of the Guild of Youth club name when reporting the results of the sports day. See *Daily Worker*, 28 April 1930.

43. *Daily Worker*, 8 April 1930. BWSF National Committee report, n.d. (NMLH). The gala included French and German contestants, although the limitations of the BWSF are perhaps revealed by the fact that two German comrades complained to the RSI following the gala (BWSF Sub Committee minutes, 24 October 1930, NMLH). What the complaints were is unclear, but they were repudiated by the BWSF.

44. *Daily Worker*, 27 February 1931.

45. Jones, 'Sport', p.166.

46. For example, the BWSF football team that visited the Soviet Union in 1927

played in front of 35,000 people; Jones, 'Sport', p.159.

47. Despite the fissure that emerged as a consequence of the communist 'take-over' of the BWSF, the federation was never an exclusively communist venture. Overt sectarianism was condemned whenever it was noted (BWSF National committee minutes, 7 June 1931) and even at the height of 'Class against Class', ILP football teams and non-party members participated. Indeed, the BWSF National Conference of 6–7 December 1930 resolved that the BWSF open to all clubs whether Labour Party, ILP, trade union or factory based. (BWSF National Congress report, 6–7 December 1930, NMLH). That said, some workers on Tyneside were reported to 'fear the club was run by the Communist Party', and the Bow West Ward Labour Party football team withdrew from the London Cup in 1928 because of the BWSF's communist connections.
48. MacColl, 'Theatre, Manchester' in Samuel, MacColl and Cosgrove, *Theatres*, pp.224–5.
49. Samuel, 'Theatre', p.50.
50. Thomas, 'Theatre of Struggle'. Thomas insisted that 'the old naturalistic stage-setting has been abandoned' and subsequently, a 'new season' of the WTM opened in September 1930, touted as the 'new season commencing on new lines'; *Daily Worker*, 30 August 1930. See also 'Trudnik', 'Workers' drama—a weapon in the class struggle', *Daily Worker*, 11 January 1930.
51. For the latter, see R. Waterman, 'Proletet: The Yiddish speaking group of the Workers' Theatre Movement', *History Workshop*, no.5 (1978).
52. *Daily Worker*, May 1931. Towns represented included Nottingham, Sheffield, Barnsley and Doncaster.
53. 'Basis and development', *Theatres*, pp.99–105.
54. R. and E. Frow, 'The Workers' Theatre Movement in Manchester and Salford, 1931–1940', *North West Labour History Group Journal*, no. 17 (1992–93) p.68; MacColl, 'Theatre, Manchester' pp.233–8.
55. E. MacColl, *Journeyman. An autobiography* (London, 1990) p.207, 'Theatre, Manchester', p.138: '[T]o stand on top of that truck and sing and perform for your own people—it was the most magnificent experience…it was what the theatre should be.'
56. 'Basis and development', p.102.
57. The ILP-sponsored Masses Stage and Film Guild was more traditional than the FWFS and stage tended to take precedent over film. No productions were initiated, and distribution was limited. See Hogenkamp, *Parallels*, pp.39–41.
58. Henry Dobb ('Aubrey Flanagan'), *Sunday Worker*, 23 September 1928. Also quoted in Hogenkamp, *Parallels*, p.28: 'And at any rate the Film Society with its minimum subscription of twenty-five shillings is not for the class for whom the Russian workers' productions were made.'
59. For such complaints by the Birmingham WFS, see *Daily Worker*, 7 October 193, cited in Jones, *Film*, p.172. Also, with regard to the London WFS, *The Worker*, 16 May 1931. The subscription to the Salford WFS, which was reliant on the Salford Social Democratic Land and Builders' Society, was 8s. per season, ris-

ing to 10s. in 1933. The entrance fee in 1930–1 was 6d. An annual loss was subsequently incurred, although the society continued until the end of the decade.

60. Hogenkamp, *Parallels*, p.50.

61. *Ibid.*, p.82; *Daily Worker*, 3 August 1933.

62. The Minority Movement had been involved in the FWFS' conception. Jones, *Film*, p.168. This was facilitated by the fact that both the London and Salford WFS emerged in conjunction with trade unionists. For Salford, see R. Cordwell, 'Workers' Film Society', undated cutting (WCML).

63. *Daily Worker*, 14 April 1930; For example, the Liverpool WFS, through the Co-operative society, was able to screen *Turksib* (about the building of the Turkestan-Siberia railway).

64. From June 1931, the Manchester and Salford Workers' Film Society. For a case study, see Jones, *Film*, pp.172–7; *Daily Worker*, 23 September 1930 and 15 May 1931. At the first annual conference of the FWFS in September 1930, societies were listed in Bradford and Cardiff.

65. See for example, *Daily Worker*, 28 February 1930 for a report on the screening of the Soviet *CBD* at the Atlas cinema, London, with a Laurel and Hardy comedy. The 'cultural' films had such titles as *Autumn Mists* and were not always well received by audiences keen to see 'the struggle'. P.J Poole, in a letter to the *Daily Worker*, 28 May 1930, called them 'sentimental, meaningless rubbish'.

66. *Daily Worker*, 7 July 1931.

67. Jones, *Film*, pp.173–4.

68. In particular, Atlas' own supplier, Weltfilm in Germany, closed down, while the transition to sound films, or 'talkies', prompted an initial dearth of Soviet product.

69. CPGB St. Pancras Local annual report, 1926–27 (Pollard papers, Bodleian Library). Twenty-one dropped out and the remaining three failed to turn up for the exam; *Communist Review*, January 1931. Non-party workers accounted for 197 members of the Workers' Study Circles.

70. *Ibid.* Liverpool did have five Workers' Study Circles, however, comprising 50 members (all party). Other figures include: South Wales, 14 members in the District School and 62 workers in nine study circles (22 non-Party); Birmingham, 12 members in the District School and 25 members (all party) in one study circle; Bradford, 18 members in the District School and 40 members (all party) in two study circles; Tyneside, 16 party members in the District School and 75 workers in four study circles (25 non party). Scotland had 20 party members in the District School.

71. *Party Training* (Dutt papers, WCML). Scotland recorded the biggest increase with 25 study circles comprising 202 party and 78 non-party members. In South Wales, the number of non-party members (63) attending 11 study circles was greater than the number of party members (60).

72. *Daily Worker*, 23 March 1931.

73. *Outlines for Students and Party Trainers* (London, 1931). In 1932, the Party issued *A Six Lesson Outline for Local Party Training Groups* (London, 1932) which com-

prised: Lesson One. The economics of capitalism; Lesson Two. Imperialism; Lesson Three. The state; Lesson Four. Party organisation; Lesson Five. The role of the party; Lesson Six i) The Communist International ii) The Soviet State.

74. Croft, *Red Letter Days*. Moreover, there is an expanding bibliography of communist autobiographies. Of the 'lesser-known' comrades, see E. Benson, *To Struggle is to Live. A working class autobiography*, 2 vols (Newcastle, 1980); F. Deegan, *There's No Other Way* (Liverpool, 1980); M. Docherty, *A Miner's Lass* (Preston, 1992); M. Morgan, *Part of the Main* (London, 1990); L. Moss, *Live and Learn. A life and struggle for progress* (Brighton, 1979); B. Selkirk, *The Life of a Worker* (Dundee, 1967).

75. *Daily Worker*, 3 January 1931. The Esperanto club was based in West London. A St. Pancras Party social in February 1928, for example, included a performance by the Communist Orchestra, the singing of revolutionary songs (led by Rab Stewart) and a workers' theatre production entitled *The Cat Burglar. Programme for St. Pancras Local Party Committee Social*, 4 February 1928 (Pollard Papers).

76. Hogenkamp, *Parallels*, p.82.

77. BWSF National Committee minutes, 7 June 1931 (NMLH). George Sinfield criticised BWSF organisers for 'talk[ing] down to members' and 'thrust[ing] things down the throats of workers they don't want to hear'.

Changing Minds, Saving Lives
Franz Kafka as a key industrial reformer

Martin Wasserman

Everyone recognizes Franz Kafka as being one of the most significant writers of the twentieth century. W.H. Auden stated that Kafka is 'the author who comes nearest to bearing the same kind of relation to our age as Dante, Shakespeare, and Goethe bore to theirs'; and the French playwright and poet, Paul Claudel, has asserted that 'who is for me the greatest writer, there is one—Franz Kafka—before whom I doff my hat'.[1]

However, my concern in this article is not so much with Kafka the gifted writer, as with Kafka the dedicated industrial reformer. It will be argued that during Kafka's lifetime his reputation was based just as much, if not more, on the reforms he helped to enact as a lawyer with the Workmen's Accident Insurance Institute for the Kingdom of Bohemia (later Czechoslovakia), as it was on his importance as an author. This argument will be made by referring, first, to Kafka's socialist tendencies and, then, by delineating some of his efforts which led to changes that vastly improved the lives of people toiling in the Czech labour force.

Kafka's socialism

Franz Kafka grew up in a well-to-do household; his father was the proprietor of a thriving textile store in Prague. However, the father, in his position as 'boss', treated employees quite roughly, and Kafka at a very early age developed an understanding and a compassion for the abused clerical and sales personnel in the store since he perceived this group of workers as being deliberately exploited.[2]

During the years that Kafka went to school, his feelings of sympathy spread to all mistreated workers and he began to profess a great interest in socialism. Despite his shyness, Kafka even took to demonstrating his convictions by wearing the traditional red carnation of the socialists in his lapel. One of Kafka's close friends, Hugo Bergmann, who at the time was developing a lifelong interest in Zionism, even complained to Kafka that his commitment to socialism was cooling their relationship.[3]

After graduating from law school, Kafka went to Czech political assemblies to hear leaders of the socialist movement like Dr. Soukup of the Social Democratic Party and Václav Klofáč of the Czech National Socialists. He even joined a group called the 'Young Generation Club' whose members were mainly Czech socialists.[4]

When Kafka became a lawyer at the Workmen's Accident Insurance Institute for the Kingdom of Bohemia in Prague, he came into close contact with numerous cases of labour injustice in almost all the industrial towns of the region that he supervised. It was through the official reports which he wrote for this job that Kafka, firmly and precisely, expressed his socialist views about society's obligation towards its victims. Furthermore, based on his professional experiences with oppressed workers, Kafka eventually wrote the novel, *Amerika*, which many critics have viewed as a severe condemnation of capitalism.[5] The first chapter of this novel, called 'The Stoker', was even translated from German into Czech and then published in the socialist literary review, *Kmen*.[6] One commentator has gone so far as to say bluntly of 'The Stoker' that 'we would be hard put to find in literature before World War I a work of a non-proletarian author that views with such deep sympathy, and proclaims the rightness of the proletarian cause...than Kafka's'.[7]

We obtain further evidence of Kafka's opposition to capitalism from a series of conversations he had with Gustav Janouch, a young friend of his. In one conversation, Kafka proclaimed that the great evil of capitalism is that 'the luxury of the rich is paid for by the misery of the poor'. In another discussion, Kafka said of the capitalist factory system that it is merely an institution for increasing financial profit and, as a result, workers have a subordinate function, being 'an old-fashioned instrument of economic growth, a hangover from history, whose...skills will soon be replaced by frictionless thinking machines'. In Kafka's harshest criticism of capitalism, he claimed it was a system of dependencies, containing mutual enslavements from top to bottom. According to Kafka, inherent to the system of capitalism was that everyone and everything belonging to it was destined to be both dependent and enchained, making capitalism not only an unfortunate state of the world but also an unfortunate state of the mind.[8]

One of the persons Kafka most admired was the socialist Lily Braun (1865–1916) who, during her own lifetime, was considered quite notorious and very influential.[9] Kafka owned two books by Braun—*In the Shadow of Titans*, her family history, and *Memoirs of a Socialist*, a somewhat fictionalized autobiography which clearly expressed her militant and radical views.[10] Of the two, it was the *Memoirs* which served as an inspiration for Kafka, motivating him to write extremely favorable comments about it in letters he sent to friends. For example, in one of his letters Kafka said of the *Memoirs*: 'This life is really worth sharing. How it longs to sacrifice itself and does…How many readers would be able to recognize a success that, taken out of the context of the book, could stand on its own legs?' In another letter, Kafka, writing in even more glowing terms, asserted that: 'I am giving them away right and left. They are more appropriate for this day and age and more to the point than anything else I know, as well as being the liveliest encouragement.'[11]

That Kafka, like Braun, was a strong supporter of socialist philosophy can be seen quite clearly in a short piece which he wrote, in 1918, called 'The Brotherhood of Poor Workers'. Kafka's was then thirty-five years old and a dedicated adherent to forming a new integration between socialism and Zionism. He believed that traditional Jewish society was essentially socialist, since cooperation, rather than competition, had always been the historical ideal for Judaism.[12] Accordingly, Kafka wrote 'The Brotherhood of Poor Workers' as an indication of the type of utopian socialist society he would like to see established in Palestine when it became a Jewish homeland.[13] Among other things, in Kafka's ideal Zionist community there would be: 'Rights: Maximum working time six hours, for manual work, four to five hours. In sickness and in incapacity of old age reception into institutions for the aged and into hospitals, those run by the State. Working life as a matter of conscience and a matter of faith in one's fellow men.'[14] Not surprisingly, one critic has said of this passage that it demonstrates Kafka's positive yearning for a socialist collective which he never rejected, even in later life.[15]

Kafka's reforms

The path that Kafka pursued in order to apply his heartfelt socialist philosophy was a work-related one. It will now be shown that Kafka ultimately fulfilled his socialist sympathies through the reforms he helped to enact as a legal advisor at the Workmen's Accident Insurance Institute for the Kingdom of Bohemia.

The main function of the Workmen's Institute was to provide wage earners with insurance benefits if they suffered a job-related illness or injury. Supposedly, the creation of this organisation in 1889 was to help unfortunate workers, but its real purpose was to co-opt leaders in the labour movement who were then turning to socialism, anarchism, and syndicalism in order to obtain rights and protections for factory workers. Thus, when Kafka began employment at the Workmen's Institute in 1908, it had become a bureaucratic fiefdom which was not at all benefiting the very labour force it was mandated to help. Furthermore, the civil servants at the Workmen's Institute commonly engaged in acts of graft, embezzlement, and misconduct of office, causing the organisation to suffer from an enormous monetary deficit.[16]

One year later, in 1909, Kafka, along with the new chief administrator, Robert Marschner, and a few select executive board members, decided that reforms were absolutely necessary at the Workmen's Institute so that the organisation could fulfil its intended goal of helping any labourer who was sick or injured. Kafka, in a speech to this end, declared to all employees at the Workmen's Institute: 'Complaints...have piled up in the course of years. One thing can henceforth be taken for granted: we shall do good work. Whatever may be useful or necessary by reforms...will be done.'[17]

Even though Kafka, like Lily Braun, had strong socialist sympathies, he came to believe, also similar to the radical thinker Braun whom he so admired, that industrial reforms carried out within a non-socialist framework could serve to raise a worker's consciousness of what might be possible under socialism. Kafka harboured this belief because, having visited Czech factories on behalf of the Workmen's Institute, it quickly became evident to him that the labourers he interacted with were not revolutionaries, but sufferers. Based upon this observation, Kafka then declared: 'How modest these men are. They come to us and beg. Instead of storming the company and smashing it to little pieces, they come to us and beg.'[18] Thus, Kafka's progressive leanings were aroused through his factory visits, and he decided that he would do everything within his power, as legal advisor at the Workmen's Institute, to be of some benefit to oppressed workers.

Kafka, like any good industrial reformer, believed that if proposed changes were to prove effective, one would first have to convince all concerned parties, as well as the general public, that each sacrifice or readjustment required of them was minimal compared with the vast relief of misery that would be enjoyed by the beneficiaries of reform.[19] Consequently, Kafka took on the task at the Workmen's Institute of being public advocate for each of the reforms being enacted, since it was the approval of these changes which ultimately would serve to strengthen the well-being of the Czech labour force.

One major flaw that had to be corrected immediately was that of low insurance contributions, since employers for years had purposely underestimated their payrolls. They adopted this unethical approach because their contributions towards health and accident insurance were based on total pay-roll figures. By constant letter writing and discussions, Kafka made sure that this practice was corrected and that employers in the future would be both legally and morally obliged to state their true payrolls, thereby forcing them to contribute an accurate amount of insurance money on behalf of their workers.[20]

Also, the Workmen's Institute decided that benefits to sick and injured employees should be based not only upon payroll figures, but on occupa-tional risk factors as well. Again, it became Kafka's job to convince employers that this new procedure was definitely a more equitable way to compensate any unfortunate wage earner who, because of illness or injury, was unable to work. In this task, Kafka's persuasive abilities once more proved to be successful.[21]

At the same time as Kafka was engaged in convincing employers to take care of their workers in a just and honorable fashion, he likewise was try-ing to persuade the general public that the Workmen's Institute proposals for industrial reforms were needed to provide adequate security for sick or injured employees. Kafka fulfilled this task, first by writing persuasive arti-cles that urged the public to approve the new reforms, and then by publishing these pieces in periodicals which had fairly large circulations. For example, he concluded one of his articles intended for a broad readership with the comment: 'We readily concede that the Institute's annual reports up to 1909…offered scant reason for enthusiasm…Now things have changed…but nothing short of broad-based public support can make sure that these promising changes become permanent.'[22]

Kafka had determined quite early in his career at the Workmen's Institute that an important way in which he could be of assistance to wage earners, besides the above-mentioned job of drafting policy and publicity material about insurance compensation, was to promote health and safety issues which might result in preventing injuries or in saving lives. A major interest which Kafka had in this area was the improvement of safety features on machines so that job-related accidents might be reduced. To fulfil this goal, he attended lectures on mechanical technology, twice a week, at the German Technical University in Prague.[23] Here he learned about the design and oper-ation of machines used by the very factory workers who were insured by the Workmen's Institute.

After acquiring a thorough knowledge of the machine technology cur-riculum, Kafka then was able to formulate a new modification for wood-planing machines which he hoped would eventually save scores of workers from having their fingers amputated, especially in the rapidly growing lumber industry. However, as one commentator has observed, Kafka was being quite modest; his wood-planing modification prevented 'the amputation of entire hands at the wrist or even higher, with severing of veins and arteries, severe blood loss and even death'.[24] Kafka thereby made a significant contribution to the physical well-being of hundreds of Czech workers who at the time were considered to be among the most vulnerable members of the labour force.

Another health and safety issue which greatly interested Kafka was finding a way to reduce alcohol-related accidents. In turn-of-the-century Bohemia, the quarry owners were often also owners of the local taverns and here the miners would frequently go before and after their shifts, spending approximately one-third of their wages on alcoholic beverages. This practice led to an increase in on-the-job accidents because of inebriation, as well as contributing to the demoralisation and poverty of the miners' families. Kafka, working through the auspices of the Workmen's Institute, was able to get legislation passed which eliminated this unsavoury practice on the part of the quarry owners. As a result, the amount of alcohol-related accidents and deaths in the mining industry was significantly lessened.[25]

Yet another health concern of Kafka's was the reduction of severe emotional problems not only for workers but for the general public. He believed that this reduction could be attained mostly through the use of medical and psychotherapeutic procedures. Consequently, in 1915, Kafka, following approval from the Workmen's Institute, drafted petition letters which eventually succeeded in establishing a hospital for the treatment of neurological and psychiatric disorders. The hospital, when it first opened during the First World War, primarily treated soldiers who had been workers before the war but who were now suffering from 'shell shock'. Interestingly, in one of Kafka's petition letters he even goes so far as to state that the 'shell shock' brought on by wartime stress was comparable to many of the nervous diseases he had observed in the labour force which were caused by industrial stress.[26] When the war ended, the hospital was opened to anyone suffering from neurological or psychiatric problems. This facility, near Rumburk, was considered the first of its kind in the Kingdom of Bohemia. In October 1918, four weeks before the Armistice, Kafka was honoured by the government for the services being provided by this hospital for disabled soldiers, many of whom had laboured tirelessly as members of the prewar workforce.[27]

Within the Workmen's Institute, Kafka, from the very beginning of his career, had been known as the labourer's friend and his efforts on their behalf were generally viewed as indispensable. Kafka's immediate supervisor went so far as to state that 'without Kafka the whole department would collapse'.[28] Proof that Kafka's efforts were considered crucial for maintaining the health and safety of vulnerable wage earners is seen by the fact that when the independent nation of Czechoslovakia was established, after the First World War, he was one of the few exceptions to a decision made by the new government that all professional staff at the Workmen's Institute who were not primarily Czech speakers were to be dismissed. Kafka, whose first language was German, was not only retained but also given the added responsibility of evaluating legal aspects of all cases originating in other departments. This higher position, in turn, had a positive effect on Czech workers who filed 'recourses' against their employers, since Kafka acted according to form and tended to look sympathetically upon any case involving infirm or injured labourers. Naturally, in his usual modest fashion, Kafka had initially expressed surprise at his new situation at the Workmen's Institute, finding it to be both 'extraordinary' and 'unbelievable'.[29]

When Kafka died in 1924 at the relatively young age of forty, the obituaries in the Czech press came mostly from periodicals of the left. These obituaries extolled the virtues of Kafka's life, not only for the contributions he had made as a talented writer, but also for the significant ways in which he had tried to reduce the exploitation of distressed persons in the working class. For example, the *Communist Review* said of him: 'This writer with the gentle soul saw deeply into present-day social injustice; he loved his exploited fellow men and, in obscure but penetrating language, mercilessly condemned the rich.' The official newspaper of the Communist Party of Czechoslovakia, *Rudé právo*, described Kafka in these terms:

> He was a German-language writer of rare quality, a pure and delicate soul who held our corrupt world in abhorrence and dissected it with the scalpel of his reason. He saw deeply into the social system, the poverty of some and the power and wealth of others, and in a style full of imagination and parody launched a fierce attack on the great ones of this world.[30]

One sees from these obituary excerpts that a major consequence of Kafka's death was the loss of a decent man who sympathetically tried to fulfil the urgent and justifiable needs of an exploited Czech labour force.

When researchers and commentators write about Kafka's job at the Workmen's Accident Insurance Institute, they usually do so in a negative light because they believe the hours he spent labouring there could have been put to better use in the service of his literary efforts. Kafka, through his autobiographical writings, sometimes contributed to this mistaken impression by complaining bitterly about the arduousness of his work.

However, Kafka almost always did a competent and conscientious job in both areas. He is one of the most important writers in the twentieth century, and he was also a significant shaper of industrial reforms in turn-of-the-century Bohemia (after 1918, Czechoslovakia). Kafka, as a dedicated reformer, was able to find vital insurance compensation for oppressed and vulnerable workers who depended upon him for just settlements in job-related accidents. He also tried to do everything within his power to minimise or eliminate those health and safety problems which threatened hundreds of people in the Czech labour force who toiled daily under very hazardous conditions.

Notes

1. Both quotations can be found in Angel Flores and Homer Swander, *Franz Kafka Today* (Madison, Wisconsin, 1958), p.1.
2. Pavel Eisner, *Franz Kafka and Prague* (New York, 1950), pp.72–4. Kafka himself writes of his great sympathy for the workers who were employed by his father in Franz Kafka, *Letter to His Father* (New York, 1966), pp.55, 57.
3. Ronald Hayman, *Kafka. A biography* (New York, 1982), p.30.
4. Eisner, *Kafka and Prague*, p.50; Johann Bauer, *Kafka and Prague* (New York, 1971), pp.100–101. It should be mentioned here that the Czech National Socialist Party bore absolutely no resemblance to the German 'National Socialists' of the Third Reich.
5. For a summary of how Kafka's work experiences inspired the novel, *Amerika*, see Franz Baumer, *Franz Kafka* (New York, 1971), pp.58–62. For interpretations which view *Amerika* as a work of anti-capitalism, see Wilhelm Emrich, *Franz Kafka: a critical study of his writings* (New York, 1968), pp.276–315; Klaus Hermsdorf, 'Kafka's America', in Kenneth Hughes (ed.), *Franz Kafka: an anthology of Marxist criticism* (Hanover, NH, 1981), pp.22–37.
6. Indeed, the entire issue of the socialist periodical, *Kmen*, was devoted to Kafka's story, 'The stoker'. On this matter, see Bauer, *Kafka and Prague*, p.174.
7. Eduard Goldstucker, 'Franz Kafka in the Prague perspective: 1963', in Hughes (ed.), *Anthology*, p.73.
8. These quotations can be found in Gustav Janouch, *Conversations with Kafka* (New York, 1971), pp.103, 131, 151. For a commentary on one of the Kafka quotations (p.151), see Peter Heller, *Dialectics and Nihilism* (Amherst, Mass., 1966), pp.240–2.
9. For works on Lily Braun's life and writings, see Alfred G. Meyer, *The Feminism and Socialism of Lily Braun* (Bloomington, Indianapolis, 1985); Alfred G. Meyer, *Selected Writings on Feminism and Socialism by Lily Braun* (Bloomington, Indianapolis, 1987).
10. Klaus Wagenbach, *Franz Kafka. Eine Biographie Seiner Jugend* (Bern, Germany,

1958), p.252.

11. These quotes can be found in Franz Kafka, *Letters to Felice* (New York, 1973), pp.454, 499.

12. Ritchie Robertson, *Kafka. Judaism, politics, and literature* (Oxford, 1985), pp.157–8.

13. Max Brod, *Uber Franz Kafka* (Frankfurt, 1977), p.298.

14. Franz Kafka, *The Blue Octavo Notebooks* (Cambridge, Mass., 1991), p.56.

15. Wagenbach, *Jugend*, pp.162–3.

16. For an abbreviated history of the Workmen's Accident Insurance Institute for the Kingdom of Bohemia, see Frederick Karl, *Franz Kafka. Representative man* (New York, 1991), pp.219–24; Ernst Pawel, *The Nightmare of Reason. A life of Franz Kafka* (New York, 1984), pp.183–9. A more comprehensive history of the Workmen's Institute can be found in Franz Kafka, *Amtliche Schriften* (Berlin, 1984), pp.267–81.

17. Pawel, *Nightmare* (New York, 1984), pp.184–5.

18. Klaus Wagenbach, *Franz Kafka. Pictures of a life* (New York, 1984), p.104.

19. The stated hypothesis that an influential reformer should be able to communicate his or her thoughts in an effective manner can be found in Patrick Pringle, *Great Ideas in Social Reform* (London, 1968), pp.11–14.

20. Pawel, *Nightmare*, pp.184–5.

21. Karl, *Representative Man*, pp.219–21.

22. Pawel, *Reason*, p.184. Kafka's entire journal article, where he persuasively argues for each of the insurance compensation changes advocated by the Workmen's Institute, can be found in Klaus Wagenbach, *Franz Kafka: Eine Biographie Seiner Jugend* (Bern, 1958), pp.326–37. For another example of Kafka's writing that strongly supports the Workmen's Institute reforms, see Kafka, *Amtliche Schriften*, pp.154–62.

23. Hayman, *Kafka*, p.78.

24. Karl, *Representative Man*, p.223. The two original reports that Kafka wrote on his wood-planing machine modification can be found in Wagenbach, *Franz Kafka: Eine Biographie Seiner Jugend*, pp.314–25; and Franz Kafka, Amtliche Schriften (Berlin, 1984), pp.134–41. An English-language translation of the latter, complete with Kafka's illustrations of his safety device, can be found in Klaus Wagenbach, *Kafka's Prague: A Travel Reader* (Woodstock, NY, 1996), pp.82–4.

25. For Kafka's complete account of alcohol-related accidents in the mining industry, see Kafka, *Amtliche Schriften*, pp.243–67. A brief English-language summary of this account is given in Jan Hancil, *Kafka and Prague* (Prague, 1998), pp.15–16.

26. For the complete text of Kafka's petition letters urging the construction of a neurological/psychiatric hospital, see Kafka, *Amtliche Schriften*, pp.281–98. An English-language translation of a 1916 letter can be found in Franz Kafka, *Letters to Felice* (New York, 1973 edn), pp.580–1. Because of the political situation in Bohemia during the First World War, there was a German-nationalistic tone in Kafka's early petition letters. However, as the war drew to a close, the

letters which Kafka wrote as well as the hospital's policy on admissions and treatment, favored all citizens residing in what was soon to be an independent Czechoslavokia. On this matter, see note 27 below.

27. Bauer, *Kafka and Prague*, pp.116–20; and Franz Kafka, *Amtliche Schriften*, pp.281–94.
28. Pawel, *Nightmare*, p.188.
29. Pawel, *Nightmare*, 370–1 and 385–6.
30. Both obituary excerpts can be found in Bauer, *Kafka and Prague*, p.174.

Reviews

Books to be remembered

(1) e.e. cummings, *The Enormous Room,* New York, 1922

The name 'e.e.cummings' (which is how he normally wrote it) is related in the memory of those who know his work with poetry written with an experimental use of typography. His prose is less well known, and only this present title is likely to come to mind when his work is discussed. There has been a considerable critical appraisal of his poetry in the United States, much less so on this side of the Atlantic.

Cummings was born in Cambridge, MA in 1894, the son of a Unitarian minister who had taught sociology at Harvard before he became minister of the South Congregational Church in Boston. The family enjoyed a pleasant, middle-class life and Cummings had a happy and lively childhood. He began to write poetry when quite young and like his father he also drew and painted. In 1911 he entered Harvard, and received his BA in 1915 and his MA a year later. By this time he was influenced by the modernist writings of Ezra Pound and the 'New Art' of Matisse and Brancusi. Among his Harvard friends was Dos Passos.

In 1917 Cummings joined the Norton Harjes Ambulance Corps of the American Red Cross (in order to avoid the draft). His unit went to France in the summer of 1917. He had become close friends with William Slater Brown, a graduate of the Columbria School of Journalism and they were both increasingly exasperated by the bureaucratic attitudes of those in place above them. They had a lively month in Paris before taking up their duties, and unlike most of their fellow Americans they continued to spend most of their time off duty with French soldiers and civilians. It was Brown's description in his letters of those whom they met that caused a French censor to report a possible case of anti-war sentiment that might add up to treason. Brown was interrogated at length, and so was his close friend. Cummings refused to dissociate himself from Brown and they were both indicted for possible treasonable behaviour.

They found themselves in a detention camp, La Ferté Macé, in Orne. It was not, theoretically at least, a prison, since its inmates had not yet been convicted of any possible crime. There was a Commission every three months or so which reviewed the evidence for each of the interned, and those found guilty were moved to prison, while the individuals deemed clear of treason could expect to be released, but most usually were not.

It was the three months Cummings spent in La Ferté Macé that is the subject of *The Enormous Room*: a remarkable story of comradeship in the foulest of conditions, and horror, told in a distinctive style. Cummings wrote in a highly individualist manner that used images and models from *The Pilgrim's Progress*. Like Bunyan, Cummings discovered certain 'Delectable Mountains'—individuals who were sufficiently integrated within their own personalities that they remained basically unaffected by the filth, degradation and cruelties of La Ferté Macé.

The Enormous Room is a book which offered a composite survey of all that the anti-war generations of the years between the wars accepted in their detestation of the carnage from 1914. The bloodshed of the trenches remained in the background. What all could understand was the stupidity and ignorance of those whose power allowed them to give orders, and who were indifferent to the cruelties they allowed in their name. Le Directeur of La Ferté, whom Cummings described as the Apollyon of the camp—'a definite fiend', 'an unutterable personality'—had two immediate weapons against those in the camp. One was *le pain sec* and the other was *le cabinot*. Both could be ordered by the ordinary warders against any who disobeyed. *Le pain sec* stopped all food except two stone-hard morsels of bread per day. *Le cabinot*, much more serious, was the removal to very small dungeons, nine feet square and six feet high, with no bed or bedding, and only planks to lie on. All were damp, the three slightly below ground level—always used first— were often inches deep in water. Food, already miserable and often foul, was reduced.

The recital of horrors such as these, for persons not yet convicted, was unusual reading for most of the populations of western and central Europe, against the background of the huge numbers of the dead and wounded. In Britain, with one or two exceptions, it was only after the first decade—the late twenties and early thirties—that there was published the extraordinary spate of novels, plays, poetry and memoirs which revealed a deep and profound disillusionment with the glory of war. Popular opinion, while mostly not articulate, was however already affected with disbelief, cynicism or out-right rejection of the military and the politicians and their reiteration of the sacred duty of dying for one's country. In a book published in 1929, a German Social-Democrat (*Portrait of the Labour Party* by Egon Wertheimer) affirmed the results of his survey that anti-war and pacifist attitudes were more pervasive among the British people than anywhere else in western and central Europe. After noting that the heroism of war was still regarded by many in Europe as a positive virtue, he continued:

> In Great Britain the nation, both individually and as a whole, was inwardly less prepared for the War [i.e. 1914]. The mentality of the people under-went a more direct change than on the Continent, where every able-bodied young man was trained for war by having to serve from one to three years as a soldier...To the average Englishman the War was incomparably more upsetting and more incomprehensible...In spite of victory, Great Britain is at heart much more anxious to do anything pos-sible to ensure that such a thing shall never happen again. The romance of war, for Great Britain, is dead.

It was from within these attitudes that there came the famous Oxford Resolution of early 1933. Those who read Cummings at this time, the pre-sent writer being among them, were given a brilliant damnation of military sentiments and conventional ideas. Cummings himself because of the tire-less exertions of his father (which included writing to the President of the United States) was released after three months and was sent straight back to New York. His friend, who had been moved to prison, returned after a fur-ther two months. Cummings was for a time in bad physical shape with a serious skin infection. He went to Russia in 1931 for a month and two years later published *Eimi* (I Am). It was again a highly personal journal with very critical political undertones, and it put a barrier between Cummings and the growing number of left intellectuals in the closing years of the decade.

Cummings wrote his most interesting poetry before the Second World War and in the last two decades of his life he was increasingly recognised as an artist of considerable power. He died in 1962.

John Saville

The Enormous Room was published in Britain by MacGibbon and Kee in 1968; by Penguin Books in 1971.

Suburban dreams

Rosalyn Baxandall and Elizabeth Ewen, *Picture Windows. How the suburbs happened* (Basic Books, New York, 2000), xxii+298pp., ISBN 0-465-07045-0, $US27.50

This is a valuable addition to the small but distinguished scholarship on suburbia, a phenomenon not unique to the United States, as some of the publishers' blurb suggests, but apparently one of all the white Anglo-Saxon world. The respective chronologies of British and American mass suburbanisations are intriguingly intertwined, with first one and then the other leading the way. Its distinguished British architectural pedigree was explored by Walter Creese in 1966, and 20 years before this J. M. Richards had been the first to attempt its cultural history, in his second edition recognising its later functional and cultural transformation, which is also noticed in this book. Much of it is based on Levittown, where Barbara M. Kelly has traced in some detail the way that residents over the years customised their very basic and standardised houses.[1]

On both sides of the Atlantic, the serious study of suburban life has always had to make a stand against the deeply ingrained anti-suburb snobbery of the cultural élite, well explored (for Britain) by John Carey in his *Intellectuals and the Masses*.[2] Baxandall and Ewen admit to sharing this prejudice before they began, assuming that their setting of Long Island was a 'no place dominated by a culture of conformity and consumption' (p.xv). In the event, their study came to deal with more than the subtitle's 'how the suburbs happened'; for besides coming down to the present day, it uses interview and oral history to reveal the extent of suburbans' interaction with and shaping of their own environments—in spite of the dictatorial control that the creator of Levittown, in particular, sought to impose. This contradicts any idea of suburbs as trivial or irrelevant—on the contrary, they are part of the mainstream of US history.

The rural delights of Long Island were discovered by the super-rich in the early 1900s. In 1929 William Levitt and his sons began building for the affluent middle classes, using assembly-line methods (as he later said, 'we are not builders, we are manufacturers' (p.125)) and imposing stringent rules and prohibitions on those lucky enough to inhabit one of his houses. At this time in Britain, public housing for a working-class élite, rented from local authorities, was already well established, incorporating some of the most progressive ideas in planning, architecture, and building technology. Middle-class home ownership, which was only just beginning to take off, was aided by individual building society mortgages and catered for mainly by small firms using traditional and perhaps not very efficient techniques.

The 'American Dream' of well-designed homes (typically bungalows) standing on their own plots in quasi-rural surroundings got its start under Roosevelt's New Deal, which provided federal money for public housing and slum clearance. It drew its design ideas from the Regional Planning Association of America, whose luminaries included Lewis Mumford and Catherine Bauer, who looked to Europe, and particularly England's Garden City movement, for models of enlightened social housing. Centred mainly on New York, where a housing law of 1927 made possible some outstanding cooperative housing complexes, and following the precepts of the Garden City in using limited dividend companies, the RRPA put its ideals into practice in a number of planned settlements, previously described by the authors in this journal.[3] One of these, Greenbelt in Maryland (its name another English borrowing) was 'a community planned and administered for the enhancement of wholesome human relationships'. (p.67)

Once the Cold War and McCarthyism took over America, these well-planned settlements, sometimes trade union-sponsored and embellished with the best of modern architecture and art, were branded as 'communist'. This study, however, makes clear that many of the assumptions on which New Deal development was based made it, rather, 'capitalism with a socialist face'; for it subscribed to the beliefs also held by private entrepreneurs, and notably Levitt, that houses were amenable to mass production like ModelT Fords, while a 'Fordist' society of well-disciplined and well-paid workers would supply the incomes with which to afford and furnish them. But the mere suggestion of state-provided, high-quality housing was anathema to American capitalist enterprise, which mobilised to show that it alone could cater for mass home ownership. This was equated with democracy, while renting was identified with immigrants and undesirables, and hence with anarchism, communism and all things unAmerican.

So the possibility, after 1945, of continuing down the trail blazed by the New Deal was overturned by the Republicans, and future American public housing was confined to 'projects' exclusive to the poorest and not designed (as British council housing was at first) to develop into complete and sustainable communities. The notorious Senator McCarthy presided over five months of hearings in 33 cities, to establish that public housing was a communist conspiracy, a contention ably supported by the media in smear campaigns against the unions and skilled labour, and even the suppliers of materials. Levitt, who had close ties with McCarthy, was then able to become 'the Henry Ford of housing', one of those volume house builders who now 'emerged from the hearings as heroes who promised to lead the country out of crisis and build dream houses for all'. (p.104) Two things in particular made this possible: the GI Bill of Rights which gave veterans interest-free loans for house purchase; and 'Title VI' of the Federal Housing Agency which by allowing developers to raise loans against future, as yet unidentified, buyers 'changed the face of America seemingly overnight'. (p.123)

One of the outcomes was the postwar Levittown, in the first place 6000 'Cape Cod' rental homes produced by non-union labour on shrinking plots and with lowered standards—the proposed elimination of the basement was violently opposed by veterans storming a meeting. But very soon Levitt saw the future, and his own profits, in home ownership rather than renting, and began to build several varieties of 'ranch house' for sale. He then encouraged the tenants to purchase their homes and disposed of the remainder to a property company. He cleverly targeted his marketing on wives, who liked the design details derived from Frank Lloyd Wright, like the wall-sized, double-glazed picture windows, and found the fitted kitchens, with refrigerators and washing machines, very appealing. There was also—perhaps with an unacknowledged debt to the New Deal?—ample provision of swimming pools and basketball fields.

But though he tried to keep the same tyrannical control over people's lives as before—summarily buying up the local paper when it criticised him—Levitt's residents proved more unruly than he could have imagined. They criticised his unilateral decision to change the name of their town from Island Trees to Levittown, and they formed various associations that proved a thorn in his side. Life in Levittown began to reflect the changing experience of its maturing population: conservative and conformist in most respects, but showing nevertheless a surprising independence and activism. This was especially clear in the case of the wives, whose apparently stereotypical behaviour prompted the post-1968 new feminist critique of Betty Friedan and others repudiating marriage and domesticity. There was more to these suburban housewives than Dr Spock and Tupperware, however, for they combined and cooperated in numerous ways, gaining organisational experience and political influence—notably in Parent Teacher Associations which battled for high school integration. It is a telling point that later when, their families grown, some of these women became successful entrepreneurs in their own right, they insisted that their experience as housewives had been a crucial preparation.

Levittown was for first-time suburbans of the blue- and white-collar classes, kept securely white by its 'Caucasion only' [sic] clause for home purchasers. But some residents waanted to live in an integrated community, and as early as 1947 they formed a Committee to End Discrimination, which Levitt tried to thwart on many fronts. For British readers the book supplies graphic insights into the American phenomenon of 'blockbusting' by estate agents, which is only palely reflected on this side of the Atlantic. With huge profits to gain, agents spread panic and destabilised settled populations. One Long Island town of New Deal vintage that was completely shattered was Roosevelt, although it had originally been a mixed-race community. Its contemporary Freeport, however, defeated the ruse by setting up its own Homefinders agency, although it had a stormy and bitter period of struggles to end discrimination in the schools.

In the latest phase of its history, Levittown lost its distinctive suburban population profile and culture, becoming instead much more like the urban environment in general—not so much a suburb as a 'technoburb': part of an amorphous, decentralised, built-up environment where '"community" is something people buy and consume rather than produce, a lifestyle rather than a participatory achievement'. (p.256) The conventional nuclear family with the wife at home no longer sets the tone, and lone-parent families, gay couples, lodgers and illegal immigrants of all classes are in the ascendant. The once-innocent and hopeful suburb is then subject to all the urban ills of teenage discontent, drugs and Aids, while affluent home owners retreat to 'theme park' developments that, in the authors' view, compare unfavourably with early Levittown. They end with a plaintive refrain against such new kinds of home ownership: high-cost, escapist and ultimately anti-social—a refrain that is now often heard in Britain too.

It is a fascinating and beautifully presented story, even if at times one has to search for some of the factual details that seem called for. It is one that will interest all with a concern for the twentieth century and its aftermath.

Alison Ravetz
Professor Emeritus, Leeds Metropolitan University

1. Walter L. Creese, *The Search for Environment. The garden city before and after* (New Haven, CN, 1966). J.M. Richards, *The Castles on the Ground* (London, 1946; second edn, 1973). Barbara M. Kelly, *Expanding the American Dream. Building and rebuilding Levittown* (New York, 1993).
2. John Carey, *The Intellectuals and the Masses. Pride and prejudice among the literary intelligentsia, 1880–1939* (London, 1992).
3. Rosalyn Baxandall and Elizabeth Ewen, 'Housing the masses. Ideas and experiments in the US in the 1920s', *Socialist History 16* (1999), pp.49–63.
4. The term 'technoburb' was coined by Robert Fishman in *Bourgeois Utopias. The rise and fall of suburbia* (New York, 1987).

Women's suffrage

Cheryl Law, *Suffrage and Power: The women's movement 1918–1928* (I.B. Tauris, London, 1999) 270pp., ISBN 1-86064-478-3 £14.95 pbk.

The past decade has seen a reappraisal of the women's suffrage movement and the rediscovery of interwar feminism. Orthodox accounts of women's struggle for political emancipation focus upon the pre-war militant agitation of the Women's Social and Political Union, portray the achievement of universal suffrage as a legislative inevitability and dismiss the low profile political activism of the 1920s as the ineffectual and passionless campaigning of a divided and declining women's movement. Recent scholarship has highlighted the flaws in the orthodox perspective and produced a broader and more balanced history of the women's movement which stresses the complexity of its organisation and continuity of its objectives and activities from the 1860s through to the 1920s. Cheryl Law's study of the women's movement during the crucial period 1918–28 continues the process of reassessment. *Suffrage and Power* sketches a vivid picture of the women's movement as an evolving network of horizontally and vertically linked groups, each with its own agenda and preferred modus operandi, but united through common membership and formal affiliation in the struggle to achieve emancipation. Law provides a taste of the wide range of issues pursued by women's groups and the diverse interests and activities of individual campaigners, but concentrates upon the movement's pursuit of political and economic power.

The political manoeuvres and extra-Parliamentary campaigns surrounding the extensions to the suffrage in 1918 and 1928 have attracted rather less interest from historians than those associated with the reform legislation of 1832 and 1867. The partial enfranchisement of women in 1918 continues to be portrayed as the automatic response of a grateful government and nation. The role of the women's movement in pressing successive governments to complete the process of enfranchisement has largely been ignored. *Suffrage and Power* examines the strategies adopted by the women's movement during the period 1915–28 and assesses their influence upon government policy and the achievement of universal suffrage. The continuity of policy and personnel within the women's movement and its ability to adapt organisation and campaign strategies to changing circumstances contributed significantly to its effectiveness. Law rapidly dispels the myth that the women's movement abandoned its political and civil rights agitation at the outbreak of war. Whilst some leading suffragists temporarily deserted the women's cause, others continued to campaign for the vote, equal pay and equal moral standards and worked to protect the welfare and employment rights of women. The war undoubtedly provided a valuable opportunity for women to demonstrate their entitlement to citizenship, but in 1916, it was the timely and determined intervention of the women's suffrage societies that propelled the women's suffrage amendments onto the legislative agenda. Whilst some suffrage groups 'wound up their operations' in 1918, Law assembles an impressive array of evidence to demonstrate the continuing vitality of the women's movement during the1920s, examining not only the fight to complete the extension of the franchise and to secure the election of women MPs, but also the struggle to retain wartime advances and to improve women's economic and social position during and beyond the post-war anti-feminist reaction. Law emphasises the invaluable support provided by women MPs and argues that only the persistence and determination of the movement secured the submission of Baldwin's government in 1928.

Law explores the divisions within the post-war women's movement but tends to underplay their impact. The perennial problem of whether women should seek equality with men or the right to assert a women's perspective continued to cause friction. Whilst valuable welfare reforms were achieved, the breadth of the programme pursued by groups within the movement deflected attention from key issues. As Law points out, the women's movement's relationship with mainstream politics remained problematic. Welfare concerns predisposed many women to work with the Labour Party but this necessitated the difficult choice between class or sex loyalty. Law wends her way deftly through the complex network of women's organisations and the major strategies and campaigns of the 1920s but may lose some readers *en route*. The list of organisations included in the appendices provides useful assistance and the biographical sketches of key campaigners are an added bonus. Law acknowledges the limitations of her study. She does not discount the contribution of male suffragists—and indeed acknowledges the invaluable support of male MPs—but does not seek to explore their role in her narrative. Similarly, Law notes her minimal coverage of the women's welfare campaigns and the regional women's networks and identifies the need for further research in these areas.

Suffrage and Power provides valuable new insights into the development, problems and achievements of the inter-war women's movement and a useful survey of the political campaigns which marked the nation's progress towards universal suffrage. It is a welcome addition to the growing body of revisionist feminist scholarship which debunks many of the myths surrounding the history of the women's suffrage movement and celebrates the continuity and complexity of the struggle for emancipation. Law's study will be of interest not only to students of the women's movement but to those seeking to broaden their understanding of political process and the domestic context of war and reconstruction.

Christine Jackson
Kellogg College, Oxford

Imagining otherness

Rana Kabbani *Imperial Fictions: Europe's Myths of Orient* (Pandora Press London, 1994) ISBN 0-0444-0911-7 x+166pp., £7.99 pbk

In his groundbreaking study *Orientalism*, (1978) Edward Said brought to our attention the dialectical relationship between the 'Occident' and the 'Orient' and the manner in which the former defined and controlled the latter. In the quarter of a century or so since its publication, it has opened a field of enquiry which encompasses a broad range of academic disciplines and prompted an outpouring of studies, papers, articles, books on colonial discourse: the variety of textual/visual forms in which the western representations of the non-western customs are codified. Rana Kabbani's is one such study in which she analyses how various myths about the Orient have been created and perpetuated.

Following a brief introduction, she proceeds more or less in chronological fashion. Looking back at literary sources such as the travel accounts of the ninth centuries, and other writings throughout the middle ages and Renaissance times, she reminds the reader: 'Descriptions of distant lands peopled by fantastic beings have universally abounded, as one dominant group became able to forge images of the 'alien' by imposing its own self-perpetuating categories and deviations from the norm'. It is the way the 'Otherness' is depicted and what motivates such representations, which are the focus of her study. From the exaggeratedly different—the *extra*-ordinary beings—presented to a home readership/audience to entertain and fascinate, the depictions become ever more those of depravity and bestial brutality/sexuality in order to justify the colonisation of the Other's space for religious, political, sexual and economic domination.

The major focus of her book is on the late eighteenth and the nineteenth century which, according to Kabbani, spawned the most deliberate expressions of the East as lascivious, violent Other. It is from this period that Said has dated the birth of 'modern Orientalism'. It is no coincidence that this period also saw the burgeoning passion in anthropological and philological studies. Thus by observation and classification the individual could be reduced to one of a 'type', and by linguistic decoding of selected texts the Orient could be made to yield up her mysteries. By such methods, the Imperial imperative—of knowing the world it was in the process of conquering—could be satisfied. In her second chapter, 'The Text as Pretext', she offers a detailed and perceptive analysis of the writings of Lane and Burton, most particularly their contrasting 'translations' of the *Arabian Nights*. It is narrative form as much as content which is scrutinised. The 'story' in each instance is relegated to second place whilst the personal commentary of the respective translators is foregrounded. Thus, the text becomes pretext, 'the translation a mere vessel for his counterpart deliberations'. (p.44) Lane, as with his *Manners and Customs of the Modern Egyptian* (1936), presents his translation with copious footnotes and addenda conferring on his portrayals of the decadent East an academic objectivity.

Though lacking the breadth of Said's analysis of how the process of representing, indeed re-structuring, the Orient is given both legitimacy and credence under the guise of scholarly activity, this chapter provides a creditable account. The extended discussion of Burton's representation of the Orient is particularly worthy of mention. 'His' women are either lewd, wanton, lascivious, corrupting and faithless or (and here, Kabbani pertinently observes, we are talking about the 'less important ones') they are pious, prudent and virginal, or at least, not overtly sexual. As such, these representations merely re-stated the polarised patriarchal Victorian attitudes towards women but Kabbani shows how Burton's particular eroticism of the East went further: the Eastern woman was caught in a double bind—inferior because of gender and race. The blatant misogyny was rendered more acceptable to the Victorian reader: the inferior women were afterall, foreign women, their very foreignness excusing the negative representation of women. Whilst the quoted extracts confirm Burton's own predilections, they also, as Kabbani effectively argues, mirror those theories and practices flourishing 'at home': the anthropological and medical studies which 'proved' racial theories and hierarchical development; the morbid (and misogynistic) obsession with sexual disease.

Kabbani moves next to the visual representation of the Orient—more particularly to an examination of the Orientalist gaze into the forbidden harem. Indeed, the harem became a metaphor for the Orient: exotic, opulent, promising abandoned sexual passion, yet simultaneously representing corruption, cruelty and treachery. Her semiotic analyses of a number of artistic works from the nineteenth century (accompanied by photographic plates) are detailed and lucid and show how the Orient 'is caught in a state of timelessness…hushed into silence by its own mysteries, incapable of self-expression, mute until the Western observer lends it his voice'. (p.73) Here, the choice of the possessive adjective is relevant, for throughout her book, Kabbani explicitly argues that the West's view of the Orient is mediated through patriarchal discourse.

The works she selects are products, and articulate the values, of patriarchy. In this she echoes Said's monolithic treatise of some two decades earlier (though his subsequent *Culture and Imperialism* did acknowledge a feminist discourse). As such she argues fiercely and persuasively. Yet while she concedes the existence of 'notable instances' of Victorian women travel writers, she dismisses them as 'token travellers' who were forced to 'articulate the values of patriarchy'. This seems a sweeping dismissal of the achievements of the likes of Gertrude Bell, Ida Pfeiffer, Isabella Bird and others and also, from a feminist perspective, sidelines an important point: their very act of writing for publication transgressed class/gender codes and thereby demonstrates at least a partial resistance to patriarchal values.

By concentrating on the works of male artists such as Delacroix, Gérôme, Lecompte de Nouy and Ingres amongst others, Kabbani's study amply illustrates how barbaric cruelty juxtaposed against fabulous opulence becomes a recurrent artistic motif in representations of the Orient, and how the West's perception of the harem as a site of unbridled sexuality is encoded. Nonetheless, her choices privilege the male gaze and deny the existence of any non-voyeuristic gaze, indeed any alternative female discourse. In fact, as Reina Lewis[1] has recently argued, the French artist Henriette Brown, amongst others, allowed the female gaze to enter the space of the Other and thus reveal the harem's interior as a site of order and domesticity, of extended kinship—a female/child zone: a stark contrast to the illicit, sexually exploitative site connoted by the re-presentations of the male author/painter.

Writing as a Muslim feminist, Kabbani notes that nineteenth century notions of Western superiority still function as a manipulative oppressive force, particularly so in the debate about the nature of Islam and its treatment of women. She delivers a venomous attack on 'the privileged Ivy League campus feminism', which strives to 'liberate' Muslim women from their 'repression'. Such sentiments are rooted not in a first hand, lived experience of the Muslim world and its history, but are a legacy of the imperialistic writings of Lane, Charles Doughty (and later, T.E. Lawrence) who were themselves, so Kabbani maintains, merely parroting the anti-Islamic polemic of previous eras. So, as with every other aspect of Oriental

Otherness, Islam is assigned a mythical position of inferiority, not because
of what it *is* so much as what the Christian deems it to be. Whilst valoris-
ing Blunt for his championing of the East and for his sympathy for Islam
she is scathing in her critique of Doughty's writings. In a particularly detailed
textual analysis, she shows how his narrative style and archaic linguistic structures confirm the West's perception of the Orient as static, fixed in time,
unchanging and unchangeable and reveal his fanatical contempt for Islam.

With little recourse to theory, Rana Kabbani avoids the obfuscatory prose
which sometimes ensues and produces a fluent, fierce and at times polemic,
yet always highly readable account of the (mis)representation of the East.
Laudable, yet the dearth of reference to Said or Foucault amongst others is
mystifying, given that she so closely utilises the former's notion of
'Orientalism' and the latter's proposition that knowledge produces power
(and vice versa). Nonetheless, this should not detract from the fact that this
is a meticulously researched work informed by a plethora of primary literary and pictorial sources which she scrutinises closely and perceptively.
Imperial Fictions presents a highly effective and damning indictment of the
patriarchal re-presentations of the Orient. Her closing injunction to the
reader is to 'continually question the testimony we have inherited, be it from
the soldier, the scholar or the traveller'.(p.139) One way of doing just that
must surely be to examine and interpret the Orient through a multiplicity of
discourses, including the feminine, and it is a source of disappointment to
this reader that Kabbani, in an otherwise insightful study, ignores the existence of such discourses.

Kathy Burton

1. Lewis, R. (1996), *Gendering Orientalism: Race, femininity and representation*, London:
    Routledge

Creating history

Jane McDermid and Anna Hillyar *Midwives of the Revolution: Female
Bolsheviks and women workers in 1917* (UCL Press, London, 1999), 248pp.,
ISBN 1-8572-8624-3, £14.99 pbk.

This well-researched book does not claim to offer anything new in the way
of evidence about the 1917 Russian Revolutions: what it does is to highlight
the important role which women played. The authors point to the fact that
in most historical analyses women are scarcely mentioned. When there is
some acknowledgement as to the nature of their participation in the

February events, it is given in a social, rather than political, context. Women are thus generally perceived as having been motivated primarily as a result of the lack of food, and are not given credence as a serious political force intent on toppling the Russian autocracy and bringing about a new social and political order. The authors of this book set out to redress the balance, arguing that traditional interpretations of the role played by women are simplistic and flawed. The study claims that women played an integral part in the revolution—both in political and social terms.

The book does not only deal with the February revolution: a major part of it is concerned with an evaluation of women's experiences during the final century of autocratic rule in Russia. Attention is drawn to the absence of any movement towards women's political rights in the country, at a time when such struggles were being waged in other parts of Europe. The authors argue that this was not simply because both sexes were denied rights under the ruling regime, but also because critics of tsarism, whether reformist or revolutionary, thought in social rather than political terms. The woman question thus formed part of the wider debate. There are also chapters devoted to the practical experiences of working women before the First World War, brief assessments of some of the more well-known female revolutionaries, and an analysis of the participation of women in the war effort. By the end of 1915 there had been a large increase in the number of women in the urban work force, often in industries previously thought suitable only for male workers. While it is acknowledged that women workers were notoriously difficult to organise, owing to the fact that they had domestic responsibilities which men did not share, the authors point to various instances in which women can be seen to have taken direct industrial action in the form of strikes, whether for better pay or enhanced working conditions.

It is argued that women played a particularly significant part in the uprising of February 1917: indeed, they were the catalysts of the Petrograd revolution. Their actions on 23 February, International Women's Day, began with strikes and ended in looting and rioting as more and more people took to the streets. The first priority of the female strikers was to persuade all workers, male and female, to join them. Women took the lead in approaching the troops and trying to persuade them not to fire on the demonstrators.

It is important to acknowledge the contribution made by women: they have been ignored for much too long. However, to state, as the authors do, that women were the instigators of the February Revolution takes things a little too far and actually devalues the actions of the other actors involved, whether soldiers or male demonstrators. In fact, it has been amply demon-

strated in a great many studies carried out over the years, that a complex combination of factors contributed to the fall of the autocratic regime during
the February days.

International Women's Day on 23 February was marked by a procession
of people demanding bread, and equality for women. At the same time,
between 78,000 and 128,000 workers went on strike to protest about food
shortages. However, the day passed reasonably quietly, and the streets were
quiet by 10 p.m. The authorities, if unprepared for the scale of the demonstration, were nevertheless able to contain it without using force.

The situation in Petrograd deteriorated on 24 February, when 160,000—
200,000 workers gathered on the streets, leading to looting and clashes
between the strikers and the police. The crowds grew more aggressive the
following day, taking advantage of the apparent reluctance of the authorities to quell the demonstrations by force. With the majority of factories
closed, up to 300,000 workers were now involved. Revolutionary slogans
were heard, and three people were killed. The Mensheviks were already discussing the formation of a workers' soviet; the Bolsheviks, on the other
hand, were still dismissing the unrest as food riots (not an uncommon phenomenon). As late as 26 February, the Tsar and his advisers were unaware
of the gravity of the situation.

The people, who were living in conditions of economic chaos throughout the country, were desperate: the impotence of the tsarist government
compelled the masses to take decisive action. All the European nations at
war were suffering in efforts to provide their armies with supplies while continuing to maintain normal life at home. But the other countries involved all
managed to deal with the situation better than Russia did. The bourgeoisie
were weak and disorganised and wholly dependent on the autocracy, while
the workers and peasants had no rights in the tsarist state and cared nothing for it. The entire state mechanism—economic, social and political—was
in the hands of the tsarist government. The war upset this obsolete machin-
ery and led to chaos. By the beginning of February 1917 it was impossible
for Russia to continue its participation in the conflict, both in a material and
in a moral sense. Conditions of famine were seen throughout the country,
and supplies to keep the factories in the cities functioning could no longer
be procured.

The weather conditions in Petrograd in February 1917 were also particularly severe: food and industrial supplies were badly hit. Fuel shortages led
to bakeries being shut down, and rumours started to spread that bread
rationing was to be introduced. Panic buying ensued. Factories were closed,
leaving tens of thousands of laid-off workers on the streets. Nicholas II

showed that his grasp of the situation was feeble, by leaving the city.

It is certainly possible to place the blame for the onset of revolution on the Tsar, who sent a cable ordering General Khabalov, Chief of the Petrograd Military District, to open fire and put down the disorder. This illustrates the extent to which the Tsar had lost touch with reality. Certainly, he was badly advised by the people in whom he put his trust, and was not told the full seriousness of the situation. However, this cannot be seen as a defence for his action. It was, after all, the job of his advisers to fully appraise him honestly about the true situation; equally, it may be argued that Nicholas II, as Tsar (with all such a position entails) should have made it his business to be aware of what was happening in his own country. Once the order to fire on the demonstrators had been sent, it could not be rescinded and on 26 February, the police and soldiers opened fire on the crowds who again massed on the streets.

The day proved a turning point. Demonstrators descended on the barracks of Pavlovsky Regiment and shouted that the soldiers had been firing on the people. This led to mutiny in the ranks, as the soldiers—themselves peasants and workers, brothers and cousins of the rioters—joined them. The mutiny of the Petrograd garrison turned the disorders into full-scale revolution. The tsarist authorities therefore had no military control in the capital. Soldiers helped to organise the crowds and gave them directions. Soldiers and workers captured the Arsenal and armed themselves, then took over the other major arms factories. Understanding the importance of communication links, they quickly occupied the telephone exchange and many railway stations. Other demonstrators turned their attention towards the police, attacking their buildings and destroying records, before moving on to the prisons and releasing inmates.

Tsarist police reports evaluated the strength of popular unrest in the country as far greater than that seen during the events of 1905. The demonstrations were a spontaneous reaction to the shootings of 26 February, and developed into open warfare against the ruling regime.

However, the book does offer a new perspective on the events. The authors conclude with a brief reminder that the participation of women in the 1917 revolutions did little to change the persistence of patriarchal attitudes and practices in the Soviet Union. Nevertheless, the important and integral part which women played in the overthrow of the autocracy should not be ignored.

Terry Mayer
Birkbeck College

Possible futures

Pantich, L. and Leys, C. (eds) *Necessary and Unnecessary Utopias: Socialist Register 2000* (Merlin Press, London 2000) 297+xi pp 0-8503-6487-6 £12.95 pbk.

The *Socialist Register* for 2000 is constructed around the theme of utopia. The theme is perhaps only loosely kept to at places, essays ranging from Norman Geras's unashamedly utopian speculations on utopia to Peter Gowan's meticulous deconstruction of NATO's policy on Kosovo. Some of the essays make for interesting reading, particularly the latter and Judith Hellman's piece on the 1994 uprising in Chiapas; while Terry Eagleton's piece is witty and a pleasure to read. However, here I will focus on two other essays in the collection; Alan Zuege's 'Chimera of the Third Way' and Ricardo Blaug's 'Outbreaks of Democracy'.

Zuege's piece evaluates a variety of social democratic attempts to steer a path between old-fashioned, post-Second World War social democracy and neo-liberalism—or, in other words, various interpretations of the 'Third Way'. The first part of the essay provides a cogent and useful summary of three distinct positions—'supply-side corporatism', 'open-economy corporatism' and 'the case for corporatist social governance'. What unites these different approaches is their advocacy of 'corporatist' arrangements for social and economic governance, or more broadly speaking the construction of institutions that would facilitate pluralist negotiation and compromise between different social and economic actors—the state, workers in the public and private sector, private capital investors, users and providers of welfare services and consumers. Yet these institutions, their advocates recognise, cannot be built on the foundation of old-style corporatism—a mass and fairly uniform system of industrial production and state-led Keynesian demand management. These characteristics of Western European societies having vanished for good, new strategies must be adopted to re-invigorate social democracy.

Whilst Zuege is balanced in his presentation of these various versions of the third way, the second half of the essay is relentlessly hostile to them. He rejects the idea that corporatist governance in post-Second World War European social democracies facilitated social peace and affluence. Rather, corporatism encouraged social conflict and industrial militancy, to the extent that capitalists, in alliance with the state, ushered in a period of rapid technological change, industrial restructuring and a neo-liberal global economic order 'to unleash downwards pressures on workers' (p.98). The solutions offered by the outlined versions of the third way are then, one by one, dismissed. Supply-side corporatism falls because the growth in production it seeks to stimulate cannot be absorbed in global conditions of excess capacity and weak demand. Even if it could, there is no reason to accept that the gains for individual nations would be distributed on a socially equitable basis (i.e. capitalists would grab the lion's share), and the non-competitive would fall even further behind. Open economy corporatism—which supports social compacts to secure long-term growth, partly through voluntary wage restraint—faces the same sort of problem. In conditions of austerity and economic deflation, incomes policies are likely be used by capitalists to reduce costs and maximise profits. As for corporatist social governance—which aims to foster a range of secondary associations in which there is widespread citizen participation—it is unrealistic and can only promote bureaucratic and state-capitalist interests.

All of the examples of third ways examined by Zuege are considerably more radical than anything signed up to by Blair, Schroeder or Clinton. He is right to point out that, in the current political and economic climate, it is unlikely that most of what is offered here in the 'radical' third way could be achieved. But Zuege's substantive criticisms are based on an image of the world in which capitalism is monolithic, and in which well-meaning social democrats end up doing the dirty work for capital by cooking-up schemes which meet the requirements of the neo-liberal global order quite nicely. Not only does this deny, in the face of a substantial body of evidence, the significant gains that social democracy has won for working-class people in Europe since the Second World War, but it also leaves us struggling to do anything but stand carping on the sidelines. And indeed, this is exactly what Zuege wants: all we need to do is wait for a repositioned social democracy to show itself a stooge of capitalism and then we can put 'real alternatives' back on the agenda. The problem is to be clear what in practice, these alternatives might be.

Ricardo Blaug's essay attempts to chart the emergence, development and dissolution of radical democratic movements. He takes democracy to mean a 'mode of being' (the phrase is Sheldon Wolin's), rather than an institutional blueprint, in which people organise to oppose currently constituted states of affairs. Democratic movements 'burn brightly, then either fizzle, are repressed, become profoundly unfair, or are co-opted and institutionalized'. (p.153) Central to the process of dissolution is the development of what Blaug describes as a 'secondary layer of structure', made up of specialists, which tends to dominate the movement as a whole, and becomes gradually more isolated from its ordinary members. This institutionalisation of the movement is, Blaug thinks, a prelude to its renunciation of radicalism in favour of compromise with the existing organs of the state.

Blaug provides us with a useful sketch, but less on why it is that originally participatory movements either die or eventually develop a system of representative, specialised leaders. There is perhaps a lack of precision here, in defining terms, which unfortunately affects the pieces generally. For example, under radical democratic movements Blaug includes those responsible for the revolutions in eastern Europe, striking miners' wives, and those Liverpudlians who boycotted the *Sun* after the Hillsborough disaster. But, on Blaug's understanding of outbreaks of democracy, we could also include here lynch mobs, people who picket abortion clinics, and racists protesting against immigration. This makes us less likely to see radical democratic movements as axiomatically good.

Arguably, what Blaug is talking about could be interpreted as unorganised collective action in support of some or other goal. Historically, this type of action has been important, but wherever it has dominated political life its effects have tended to be disastrous—it creates chaos, which is usually resolved by highly authoritarian rulers taking power and crushing dissent. Indeed it might be argued that it is not the case that the crowd is democratic because it involves mass participation—within participatory movements there are always a small number of orchestrators and a large number of followers. The mechanisms which determine the emergence of Blaug's second layer do not obtain solely, or even most importantly at the level of overt political manipulation of democratic action. Where popular participatory movements do become institutionalised, this is largely due to the individual and social unconscious. Popular political movements face a 'choice': retain their 'spontaneous' character and abandon any realistic hope of achieving their goals; or develop an organisational apparatus that improves its effectiveness, even if this requires some compromise of its principles.

None of this means that current levels of popular participation in the politics of liberal democracies are normal or necessarily acceptable. But Blaug, it seems, is highly suspicious of any attempt to extend participation at local levels while retaining representative democracy at the level of the state. Unfortunately, Blaug offers no alternative course of action. In this, Blaug's essay represents the greatest problem for writers on the theme of utopias. History is replete with examples of failure, such that now we have a catalogue of how utopia will not be created. In such circumstance it is not realistic to imagine that one book of essays will find ways through the blockages, where so much thought and practice has previously failed.

Jason Edwards
School of Politics and Sociology, Birkbeck College, London